Tahiti Origin

The Journey to the Pacific, a History

Author

Ade Pearson

Copyright Notice

Copyright © 2017 Kenneth Wilson Printing
All Rights Reserved

All rights reserved. No part of this book may be reproduced or transmitted in any form or by any means, electronic or mechanical, including any information storage and retrieval system, without written permission of the publisher

First Printing: 2017.

ISBN: 978-1-912483-71-6

Publisher: Kenneth Wilson Printing.
Main St, Harome, near Helmsley YO52 5JE
Harome
Yorkshire
United Kingdom

Content

Introduction 1
Tahiti Origin 3
   The Journey to the Pacific.. 3
The Raining of Early Tahiti 48
   The Original Tahitian: Ancestral Traits B.C........................... 48
   Early Face of Tahitian in Humanity - Nature A.D.................. 86
First Contact with the Explorers 110
   The Missionaries, 1797.. 147
   Turmoil: the Old Order Changes - 1815............................. 149
Tahiti Bourty 156
The Tahitian Royal Family....................................190

Introduction

Little introduction on Tahiti environment, our main focus is on Tahiti early stage, why Tahiti and how this people came about, and become what they are today, the people that made up Tahiti as one of different islands. The island of Tahiti upon which the Tahitians lived is the largest of the Society Islands and is located in the windward segment of that group at 149°30' W and 17°30' S. It is a high island of volcanic origin with peaks rising above 1,500 meters.

The mountainous interior is covered with Forest and ferns while the lower slopes, especially on the leeward side, are brush and reed covered. In the inhabited valleys and coastal plains open stands of indigenous trees and tall grasses were scattered between the cultivated fields of the Tahitians. Wild fowl were said to have been relatively scarce and limited to a few species, pigeons and ducks being specifically mentioned. Wild four-legged creatures were limited to a few small lizards and the Polynesian rat, the latter probably brought by Polynesians

Tahiti Origin

The Journey to the Pacific

With powerful arms the Tahitian grasped the shaft of his adze and swung the stone axe high over his head. Pausing only for a fraction of time to determine precisely where the blow would land, he thought it down, cutting an arc through the sun. When the blade landed splinters flew across the humid air, tinging it with the sweet smell of sap. The canoe would be months in the making. For the great voyages it would undertake, only the finest tamanu or ati wood, the strongest coconut-fibre twine and true love for the perfection of its smooth hull, polished with the skin of sharks, would ensure success - and perhaps the discovery of new lands. The lightweight wood of hibiscus trees would furnish the paddles, and ironwood that grew along the coast had already made the stem posts.

When finished the canoe would have twin hulls 21 metres long, and a platform in the centre with a thatched shelter. It would support some sixty men, women and children, plus pigs, dogs, chickens and many other provisions. it was not always easy to predict how long the voyages would last, but with fish and turtles caught from the sea and a fair breeze, a great distance could be covered in a week. Chiefs would come from far and wide to commission their craft for the long voyages between islands. Huahine was the home of the master canoe-builders, only those of the nearby island Raiatea could rival them. The skill of centuries rested here.

The canoe-building site was near to the shore. Teams of warriors would drag the huge double-hulled canoe on log rollers over the sand at the to of the beach, to the pass through the reef and out into the sea at high tide. Only war canoes were larger; they could exceed 35 metres and hold as many as 300 warriors ready for battle. At their launching it was customary to sacrifice slaves and throw their blood over the timbers, or place the live bodies of enemies between the rollers as the canoe was dragged to the sea. The construction clearing was filled with the sound of falling adzes.

There was a smell of molten breadfruit sap to be used for caulking the wood. Women were cutting the huge leaves of the fara palm into strips to weave them into sails and teasing fibres from coconut husks for twine. From time t tome the chief would come by to inspect the work, carrying his carved staff and wearing a large whale's tooth around his neck to indicate his high rank. His hut was not far away, its roof newly thatched with grasses gathered from the hillsides inland. Each year they burned the hills; that way the grasses grew better, and it kept the forest back. most had been cleared from the lowlands and valleys now. Further up the coast was the chiefly village of Maeva, a whole string of stately residences positioned around a pleasant inland lagoon. On the hillsides there were other houses and many marae in which to worship the gods. Before work had begun on this canoe, the carver's tools and those of all the other pahi canoe-builders had been dedicated to Taaroa, the father of all gods, at the marae. A great feast of whole roasted pigs had followed, and the high priest had made offerings to the god of beauty and good weather, Tane.

On the day of fa'ainuraa i te vaa the craftsman of the new canoe would sing a simple prayer song:

> *If I sail my canoe*
> *Through the breaking waves,*
> *Let them pass under,*

*Let my canoe pass over,
Tane!*

Small blue lorikeets screeched their high pitched 'schee-schee' between the tall palms which shaded the site. Above, white-tailed tropic birds wheeled in the sun. The first inkling that something was wrong was a strange roaring sound coming from the reef, almost like the rumbling of thunder. The men stopped their work and looked about; there were no clouds, no signs of a storm. Then suddenly there was a great cry of 'Are miti rahi' from the beach, the sound of children screaming in fear, and men and women came running through the low bushes on the shore.

A vast wall of water rushed up the beaches, smashing the fringing ring of palms like matchwood, and as the canoe-builders turned to run they could see it clutching over them. The chief's hut and all the others in the village nearby were swept before the advancing sea, carried inland in a mass of broken tree limb, soil, sand,

and floating debris. When the waves receded and drained back into the sea, the canoe-builders' site had vanished beneath a wasteland and mud as if it had never been.

Out in the deep ocean, tidal waves move at incredible speeds, 400 kilometres an hour or more is not unusual, but because of the great volume of water there they result only in a series of quite shallow swells. They are caused by the ocean floor collapsing after a volcanic eruption or by the Pacific plate moving into one of the deep trenches which surround this great ocean and causing an earthquake. Once a tidal wave approaches shallow seas, the pressure wave slows as it drags across the bottom and is deflected up towards the surface sometimes building to an enormous height. Then it will race across reef flats and engulf whole coastlines with millions of tons of water. Following Krakatoa's eruption in 1883, 32,000 people lost their lives in tsunamis.

In 1972 a hotel construction crew began dredging a large pit near the coast on Huahine, one of the Leeward islands in the Society group, 180 kilometres from Tahiti, capital of French Polynesia. The site was half a kilometre from the picturesque village of Fare, the capital of Huahine, situated on the west coast beside the Ava Mo'a pass which provides access from the harbour through the reef to the sea. with the first few scoops a number of curious wooden and bone objects were found which appeared to have been made by man. Fortunately, Yosihiko Sinoto, one of the most accomplished archaeologists in the Pacific, happened to be reconstructing an ancient Tahitian meeting house at the now ruined village of Maeva further up the coast. The hotel architect, Richard Soupene, invited him to take a look at the finds. When Yoshi, as he is known, first saw one bone artefact, he was stunned. It was a patu hand club, shaped like a short paddle and fashioned from whale bone. Nothing like it had ever been found before outside New Zealand.

Here at last was evidence which corroborated ancient oral legends of the Tahitians; evidence that New Zealand was colonized by Polynesians who had sailed from the Leeward Islands many years before. The site uncovered at the hotel was clearly of enormous significance. Extensive excavations followed in 1974 and 1975, during which numerous artefacts were unearthed dating back a thousand years. It also became clear that much later the site had been engulfed with mud and sand, perhaps from a large tidal wave, and an arc of deposited stones revealed the direction from which it had come. There were basalt adzes, stone scrapers and choppers, chiesels made from Terebra shells and turtle bone, and a large collection of shell scrapers and graters, as well as intricately carved fishhooks of mother-of-pearl. A wooden bow indicated that the aristocratic sport of archery was practised. There were whale-tooth pendants as worn by those of high rank, and even a chief's staff.

In 1977 there was another amazing discovery. Further dredging turned up more wooden artefacts including the boom of an outriggers. Sinoto begged for dredging of the site to be halted until further funds could be raised from the National Geographic Society. The hotel agreed. New archaeological work began and discovered a large steering paddle, smaller canoe paddles, an unfinished canoe-bailer, and two large wooden planks seven metres long. The first remains of a Polynesian long-distance voyaging canoe had been unearthed. From the positions of the finds it appeared that they had been deposited in the backwash of the tidal wave. Mud had protected the wooden artefacts from decay.

They can be seen today in the Bishop Museum in Honolulu, and bear witness to an important canoe-building site. In cook's day the people of Huahine and Raiatea were well known as master builders of long-distance voyaging canoes. The discovery of storage houses, probably for yams, at the site indicated a prosperous people, producing more than their daily needs so that some could specialize in skills other than farming. Adze-making workshops and shell-scraping sites were also found. A community of perhaps 200 people had lived here, and the large number of beautifully carved pearl-shell products suggests that they were probably involved in trading these goods to other areas.

The site revealed a people with complex social organization, a society well equipped for life on the islands and with the necessary tools to voyage great distances between them. Polynesian navigators were crossing the Pacific long before Europeans even thought of exploration. While the Greeks were felling the walls of Troy, Polynesians had already reached Fiji in their double-hulled canoes. Their voyages were far greater even than those of the Vikings.

Who were these men? Were they North American Indians or from the ancient mountain civilizations of the Andes as Thor Heyerdahl would have us think? Did they come from south-east Asia, island-hopping their way east as most other archaeologists and anthropologists now believe? Today we are closer to a final answer than ever before, due to great advances in three areas: linguistics, blood protein analysis, and archaeology. By examining the use of similar words and sounds in different island groups it is possible to see common ground between peoples widely separated by the sea, which provides clues as to the historical links between them. James King, Second Lieutenant aboard the Resolution during Cook's final voyage wrote of the Polynesians:

It cannot but strike the imagination, the immense space through which this nation has spread, the extent of its limits exceed all Europe, and is nearly equal to Africa, stretching in breadth from A'toui (Kauai) to New Zealand ... and in length from Easter Island to the Friendly Isles (Tonga) ... All the isles in the intermediate space are by their affinity or sameness in speech to be reckoned as forming one people.

The word 'eye' in Tahitian is mata, in Hawaiian maka, in Maori mata. Likewise 'person' is, in the same order, ta'ata, kanaka, and tagata. In addition many words are borrowed from one language group by another, dependent upon the contact that exists between them. In the same way as le weekend is now part of French, the Fijian word for pig, puaka, was borrowed from the Tongans, who regularly used it to describe their feasts when they had conquered parts of eastern Fiji. Tongan loan words can even be found in kava and yam festivals as far away as Pohnpei in Micronesia. It is important for the linguist to distinguish between those words that are indigenous and those which are merely loaned in establishing the true language of any island group. Language, of course, evolves with time. Its changes are a valuable tool for the detective. by careful reconstruction of ancient forms of speech it is possible to trace the proto-languages which gave rise to those spoken today and this has been enlightening in tracing the origins of Pacific peoples.

It seems that a proto-Polynesian language, with root words common to most areas, links all the islands of the Polynesian triangle ranging from Hawaii to Easter Island to New Zealand. But there are many other small island communities outside the triangle which also share this language: the so-called Polynesian Outliers. These have been discovered in Melanesia and Micronesia in the Loyalty Islands to the Carolines. Because this language shows remarkable similarity across its range, it seems that the original community which spoke it dispersed in relatively recent times. Polynesian can itself be traced back further to a much more widespread language base known as Austronesian.

With over 500 daughter languages, this is the largest well-established language family in the world, linking places as far apart as Madagascar, Indonesia, Taiwan, the Philippines, parts of Indo-China and the Malay Peninsula, right across the Pacific to Eastern Polynesia. Only in some of Eastern Indonesia, mainland New Guinea, and parts of the Bismarck Archipelago, the Solomons and the Santa Cruz Islands are non-Austronesian languages spoken. Though they are not all related these are collectively known as Papuan.

All this evidence together suggests a gradual movement of Austronesian-speaking peoples from Indonesia through the Melanesian islands and out into the Eastern Pacific. A proto-Oceanic language seems to have develop0d in New Guinea and parts of the Bismarck Archipelago, with proto-Eastern Oceanic on Vanuatu, parts of Micronesia and Rotuma. Proto-Central Pacific evolved in the Fijian Islands, giving rise to proto-Polynesian. Shared proteins in blood, and in particular blood antigens, substances which stimulate the production of antibodies, also point to relationships between peoples. The incidence of genetic diseases passed from one island group to another, such as the inherited blood disorder beta-thallasaemia, allows biochemists and geneticists to trace the origins of peoples. All of these, along with most of the animal and plant species inhabiting the islands, point to a Western origin for Pacific Islanders. It is, however, to the historian and archaeologist that we must turn for the most compelling evidence of the origins of man in the Pacific, and here there has been much controversy.

Sixteenth-century explorers were not impressed by the Polynesian sailing canoes, believing them quite incapable of bringing the islanders to their islands. The belief in a great Southern Continent as the source of Pacific peoples continued through generations of European explorers.

Over forty thousand years ago the first hunter-gatherers were walking the hills of New Guinea, then joined to Australia by land due to a lowering of the sea. In New Guinea's highlands some of the world's earliest agriculture later developed, but these primitive peoples seem to have lacked wither the skill or the desire to meet the challenge of the Pacific. Some could manage short distances between islands floating on logs, and they may have owned simple rafts or canoes, but the coloniziation of the Pacific had to wait for three innovations, these were brought by a different people who had developed them in the islands of Indonesia, the early Austronesians.

First they had perfected the domestication of certain food plants they had discovered in their rainforests; secondly they had improved ways of capturing food from their reefs and lagoons and thirdly they knew how to design ocean-going crafts capable of long-distance voyages. These people were the first humans to set foot on the Pacific's enchanted islands. In their passing they left many scattered signs; footprints that only archaeologists can discern of shell, bone, charcoal and pottery, the last of these has been crucial in uncovering the coming of man to the Pacific.

A remarkably uniform red earthenware known as Lapita with characteristic stamped designs, has been most important. Its simple appearance belies its great age; the earliest found example dates from about 1600 BC. The exact origins of the Lapita culture remain a mystery but its pots are scattered across the Pacific from New Britain and the northern coast of New Guinea to the great island of New Caledonia, across the island chains of the Solomons and Vanuatu. Its people must have sailed the 850 kilometres of ocean to Fiji, and lastly to Tonga and Samoa where their pots are also found. here, at the gateway to Polynesia, the Lapita people apparently lost their pots, for they are found no further east.

It may that the clay needed to make them was in short supply, or that a preferred form of cooking, such as the underground oven in common use today or the use of hot stones, made them obsolete. By the time Christ was born only simple pots were being made and by AD 300 their manufacture had ceased completely. distance made regular two-communication with this people's homeland to the west virtually impossible; isolated in the great islands of Fiji and Samoa and the atolls of Tonga a new culture with a new language began to develop. new tools such as basalt adzes, worked from the new volcanic rocks they found, enabled them to fashion finer canoes, and with that came a new mastery of the sea. In Fiji and Samoa over 2,000 years ago the first Polynesians were being born, and the final colonization of Oceania could begin.

It has long been believed that the Polynesians sailed directly into the Pacific from some region outside it. This now seems unlikely. The ancestors of the Polynesians were the people of the Lapita culture whose lost homeland was perhaps in the Bismarck Archipelago to the north of New Guinea, but the evolution of their culture into that of the Polynesians can now clearly be seen in the archaeology of Tonga and Samoa over the last 3,000 years. Crucial to further migration was the development of sailing craft capable of sailing upwind and so more effectively heading into the trades which predominantly blew against them from the east.

Did the Polynesians embark on their migratory journeys on purpose or were the islands merely reached by accident? Computer simulations of random drift voyages show that chance alone cannot account for the numerous colonizations that occurred. Archaeological discoveries also point to carefully planned expeditions, taking a wide range of plants and animals intended to be of use on arrival. The Polynesians had every intention of making land; it was almost as if they somehow knew that new territories lay ahead. what could have given them such remarkable confidence? Perhaps one answer is their attitude to the sea. To most Westerners, the sea is traditionally an adversary to be feared. To Polynesians it is home, more so than the land. The sea is to them a natural highway, supplied with ample food if you know how to catch it, which they did.

Another reason for the Polynesians' confidence was that they had become masters of navigation. They could read the stars and memorized star maps prior to voyages, they understood the patterns of waves caused by islands beyond horizons; they knew how to interpret drifting vegetation, flight patterns of seabirds and the warmth of currents, perhaps even gaining clues from the kinds of fish they caught. Few people have such knowledge now. Only on Satawal in Micronesia is the wayfinding art still practised by one or two ageing men.

There are time of the year when the trade winds do not blow adversely. The wind pattern reverses for a week or ten days and at these times the early voyagers could set out in their canoes knowing that the prevailing winds would soon return and bring them safely home again of no land had been found. Westerly winds tend to blow for about a third of the year in Samoa and a little less than a quarter of the year in Tahiti but occasionally they will blow for much longer, such as during the El Nino phenomenon. These intermittent westerly winds could have been responsible for carrying the first canoes to the

Marquesas, from which Hawaii and Easter Island may have been reached. The Polynesians were provided with another clue to assist them on their journeys, the importance of which has underestimated: the routes of migrating birds.

All regular seafarers not the passage of birds. They are company on a lonely ocean as well as effortlessly beautiful to watch. It may be that, like the Vikings, migrating Pacific peoples carried birds to release at sea in the knowledge that if they did not return, land must be nearby. Two birds in particular could have played a vital part in the discovery of Hawaii, New Zealand and perhaps other Pacific islands: the Pacific golden plover Pluvialis dominica and the long-tailed cuckoo. The former species migrates 9,000 kilometres each year from the tundra shores of the Russian and North American Arctic to Hawaii and then south to the Marquesas and the Society Islands. Each spring as the birds flew north to their Arctic nesting grounds, resplendent in their breeding plumage of black spangled with gold, yellow and white, the Polynesians would have wondered where they were going. The long-tailed cuckoo migrates north from New Zealand to avoid the southern winter and reaches many of the South Pacific islands including Tahiti and the cook Islands, from which New Zealand is believed to have been colonized. Their annual migration routes, observed by fisherman far out to sea, may have been a vital factor in the Polynesians' choosing a direction in which to sail.

The movement of people across the pacific came in a series of fits and starts. The origins of the Polynesians seem to lie in the genes, languages and material culture of the peoples of southern China and Taiwan, who began to migrate southwards and eastwards in about 4000 BC. Perhaps as many as 45,000 years earlier the Australoid peoples had already occupied New Guinea, but they failed to move out to the islands in any numbers. The Lapita culture developed in island Melanesia in around 1500BC. The next 600 years saw these people migrate eastwards as far as Fiji, Tonga and Samoa. In about 200 BC, they set out from Samoa and found, after a journey of 1,600 kilometres, the sharp volcanic peaks and green forested valleys of the Marquesas.

They had to adapt to new conditions. Being further north, there were fewer coral reefs here, and a shortage of fish, they experimented with new techniques to catch them. A range of bone and shell fishing gear, not seen in Western Polynesia, remains as evidence of their struggle for survival in the Marquesas. New speech, new technologies, a new culture evolved. here the Eastern Polynesians flourished for a further 500 years before three of the greatest feats of human navigation were undertaken, the ocean voyages to Hawaii, Easter Island and New Zealand. Hawaii was reached over 1,700 years ago and over 100 years later some canoes beached on the tall forbidding shores of Easter Island. The society Islands had in the mean time already been settled, and from there, in about AD 800 the prodigious journeys to New Zealand were made. A thousand years ago the great colonizing voyages to Melanesia, Micronesia and most of the other Pacific Islands were complete, and the Polynesians were the most widespread people on earth.

If human occupied New Guinea at least 40,000 years ago, already having crossed quite substantial water gaps to have done so, why does there appear to be no evidence of them in New Britain and the Solomons - a relatively short distance east - more than 4,000 years old? It seemed until very recently that man must have been landlocked in New Guinea for 36,000 years. Then in 1987 Chris Gosden from La Trobe University was excavating a cave in the centre of New Ireland overlooking the sea when he discovered evidence of man that was 32,000 years old. That so few early traces have been found in the West Pacific may be a reflection more of the lack of funds for archaeology than of man's true migration pattern in the Pacific. In the next decade it may sell be discovered that man arrived in the Solomons, Vanuatu and even Fiji far earlier than is now thought. The reason no evidence has been found may be that it lies beneath the sea, as a result of the rise in the world's sea level since the last ice age.

Much has been made of the heroic Polynesian tradition of finding islands. The discoverers were elevated to almost godlike status. what was it that made them undertake their journeys at all? overcrowding, war and banishment may have been reasons. Often it was impossible to return on pain of death, or the physical distances prevented it. Easter Island never appeared on any early Polynesian maps even through their canoes reached it, the colonizers were never able to return home to break the news. It may be that the distant ancestors of the Polynesians migrated because of a great flood. The earth began to emerge from the last ice age 18,000 years ago, and as the ice melted, the sea level rose and began to flood the lowlands which joined Australia and New Guinea, and those of the Sunda shelf which once joined the great islands of Indonesia. To move inland to avoid the encroaching se would have resulted in contact with other fierce tribes already occupying the land. Lowland people were forced into a maritime culture capable of travelling and maintaining contact between islands and living off the products of the sea. A mystery remains. The sea level rose fastest between 12,000 and 5,000 years ago, but there is no evidence of man east of the Solomons more than 3,500 years old. The reason may be that the earliest landing points now lie hidden beneath the sea.

If the ancestors of the Polynesians had embarked on their journeys prior to the rise in the sea level, the prospect of the Pacific Islands would have been far less hospitable than it is today. The lowered se level made them virtual fortresses. They were surrounded by sheer cliffs, the edges of coral reefs which had once descended beneath the ocean. Now dry and covered in scrubby vegetation, they offered few points at which to land save where the cliffs were cut by steep gorges carved by rivers draining from the mountain island. perhaps the first settlers could have inhabited caves in the coral cliffs, then walked up the steep valleys and explored the dry reef flats, covered at the time with trees. These early sites would not be found today because they are submerged and no one had cared to look for them.

It is odd that a zoologist should point out such an inadequacy to our studies of prehistory, but John gibbons was a man who moved freely between apparently unrelated subjects, forged links where none existed before, and dusted down those which had long been forgotten. Seeing how animals needed to island-hop across the Pacific, he saw no reason why the hugely increased number of islands when the sea level was lower could not have helped humans too. Before he drowned, he had been poised to investigate this extraordinary theory, first put forward by himself and Fergus Clunie, Director of the Fiji Museum.

Leaders in Pacific archaeology such as Professor John Green at the University of Auckland dismiss the idea, pointing out that the reduction in sea level did little significantly to reduce the water gaps between island groups, particularly to the west of Santa Catalina on the eastern tip of the Solomons. Still, the arguments for early settlement sites on coastlines now sunk beneath the ocean remain compelling. In Micronesia there have been reports of divers finding a cave bearing the marks of fire on its walls, and containing stones in circle like a hearth, many metres beneath the sea. Off the north coast of Australia, underwater archaeologists have found the remains of primitive houses beneath what was once the dry land of the Sunda shelf. The oldest known sites of Vanua Levu in Fiji are opposite a wide shelf over which the first settlers may have moved inland as the sea encroached.

There is growing evidence that someone had reached parts of Melanesia before the Lapita people over 3,500 years ago. Waisted axes, similar to those discovered on the Huon peninsula in New Guinea, known to be more than 40,000 years old, have been found in Bougainville, Guadalcanal, and Santa Catalina. At Poha cave on Guadalcanal in the Solomons human artefacts have very recently been discovered beneath those of the Lapita people. Santa Catalina is as far east in the south Pacific as a people with simple watercraft and moderate navigational skill could reach. Beyond, the sea formed a great divide for both man and nature On Santa Catalina today there is a strange dance still performed called mako mako. Their faces decorated with frightening patterns and wearing high conical masks, their bodies smeared with reddish clay, the men of the island silently mime an ancient legend in which 'the men of the trees', perhaps a primitive jungle folk, turn in panic as 'the canoe people' arrive from the sea. Primitive humans had almost certainly reached these islands before the ancestors of the Polynesians arrived the question is, who were they?

When the ancestral Polynesians entered the Pacific, they did not come empty-handed. The jungle fowl, ancestor of the chicken, originally wild in south-east Asia, is now wild throughout most inhabited islands of the Pacific. From their Asian homelands they also brought pigs, some still travel long distances strapped to the outriggers of canoes. dogs would also be wandering the decks of Polynesian double canoes, not intended as companions, but as food. These small brown or black dogs were an important part of Polynesian society

Their teeth would be made into decorative anklets, their hair into fringes for cloaks. The adult dogs were slothful, not hunters, but vegetarians. Often they were penned with pigs and fed on poi, a pudding made from taro roots. Once fattened they would be cooked in hot rocks and fed to chiefs, or strangled as offerings to the gods. Most valued of all were the delicious young puppies, though those that had been suckled by women, a common pracitce, were usually spared the table. The original native dog has now vanished from the Pacific, absorbed into breeds brought in by Europeans. The Pacific islands offered little for them to hunt, so they never escaped domestication to survive in the wild.

The influence of early human migrations in distributing animals around the Pacific was not inconsiderable. Possums and even tree kangaroos may have been deliberately introduced to the Bismarck Archipelago for food, as well as fruit bats to Tonga and the cook islands. Skinks and geckos travelled all over the Pacific on the thatching of shelters aboard canoes. small snakes, snails, insects and other creatures reached the islands as stowaways concealed in bundles of stored taro roots and yams. The arriving Polynesians quickly cleared coastal woodlands to grow taro, yams, coconuts, breadfruit, arrowroot, and sugar cane for eating.

The screw pine was planted around their huts for posts, and its leaves were used for mats and sails. Bamboo served a host of purposes including the making of nose flutes and stamping pipes. Lagenaria vines would grow into gourds for water, ginger was brought in and now enlivens the forest with its beautiful read flowers. There were the seeds of candle-nut trees, whose nuts would provide oil for lamps when mature, as well as Cordia seeds whose trees would offer shade, and hibiscus for flowers and paddles. The wild ancestors of all these plants grow in tropical south-east Asia, providing further evidence that the Polynesians came from here.

There is one staple of the Polynesian diet whose arrival remains an enigma: the sweet potato. Its origins lie in the high Andes and it was present - principally in Easter Island, Hawaii and New Zealand - well before Europeans could have intruded it. It may be that the seeds of the sweet potato dispersed naturally to the islands, rafting on coconuts or even assisted by birds, but the distances are immense. Another enthralling explanation is that the Polynesians may have made contact with South America. It could be that south American people, as Thor Heyerdhal believes, carried the sweet potato on their rafts to the islands, but the seafaring tradition of the Polynesians was such that their migrations eastwards need not have stopped at Easter Island. We may never know if the Polynesians reached the shores of Peru or Ecuador but if they did they would instantly have recognized the potato tuber as a root crop they could adapt to their needs and would almost certainly have returned with it, particularly to Easter Island where the cooler conditions were less favourable for the tropical crops they had originally brought with them. The geographer Robert Langdon has recently discovered early translations which reveal that manioc was also in use on the islands at the time of the first European arrivals. similar explanations may account for its presence, but the controversy lingers.

For years it has been believed that the greatest era of change to the Pacific Island environment and its wildlife began with the arrival of the Europeans. The pest animals, virulent diseases and alien attitudes they brought certainly cut a swathe across the Pacific, but in the last few years it has become apparent that the process began much earlier. Then the first Polynesians arrived they quickly imposed their cultural heritage on a yielding landscape. Forests in coastal areas were felled so that crops could be planted, soon the destruction crept into the valleys and, as population expanded, even on to the steepest mountain slopes.

The eye may be pleased by green mountains and valleys covered in low creeping Dicranopteris ferns and pink orchid blossoms mixed with patches of original forest, but these are the remnants of a ruined landscape cauterized each year by fire to provide fertile ash. Imported weeds quickly escaped and fared well on the scorched ground, defeating less vigorous endemic plants. Devoid of trees, the regularly burnt, thin volcanic soils lost goodness and slipped down slopes, spreading over river valleys and on to the reefs to create coastal plains.

Many ring forts lie beneath the mud of the Rewa valley in Fiji, lost beneath this tide of ecological change in the mountains. The increasing land on the coast could not compensate for lost land in the mountains, growing populations found themselves pressed for fertile farmland. No longer were the island evolving alone. The Polynesians had unintentionally embarked upon a gigantic ecological experiment, and its consequences were to be disastrous for the natural life-support systems of the islands, endangering the precious resources upon which the immigrants themselves depended.

Much can be leant about Polynesian eating habits by looking in their kitchens. 'rubbish pits which are centuries old can be informative. As the decades passed, the number, size and variety of shellfish on the menu declined, and there was a dramatic reduction in turtles. Certain birds became 'off', and the number of fish fell. clearly the table was becoming barer. Most dramatic of all was the disappearance of bird life. In New Zealand so much forest was lost that it was originally thought to have been the result of climatic change after the ice Age. Now it is known that the first

Maoris caused the trees to vanish, burning the landscape to plant crops and to hunt the extraordinary flightless moa. At one time there were thirteen or more species of this fascinating bird, some twice the size of an ostrich, others comparable to a turkey. within half a century of their arrival the Maori had dispatched them all, along with some twenty other species of flying bird including ducks, geese, and eagle and a crow. They also destroyed the North island fur seal rookeries.

Evidence of extinctions caused by the Polynesians in the islands of the pacific was first found at Barbers Point on Oahu in Hawaii in 1976. Yoshi Sinoto was excavating a sink hole for early human artefacts when he discovered some bird bones and sent them to the Smithsonian Institute in Washington DC for identification . The results were stunning; the bones belonged to numerous birds that no one knew existed before, including a large flightless goose and an ibis.

Snails associated with human occupation, as well as the bones of skinks and geckos introduced by man, proved that the birds existed at the time of the arrival of the Polynesians extinguished perhaps forty species of bird prior to the European explorers' ever setting foot on the land. These discoveries have not gone down well with native Hawaiians anxious to maintain the myth of the Polynesians as guardians of paradise. it may be that the Polynesians were no better conservationists than modern Westerners - although their tools of destruction were much less effective than Europeans.

Since then more evidence has been uncovered at archaeological sites on other islands. The megapodes, once wide-spread in parts of the Central Pacific, were almost certainly clubbed to death by the Polynesians or vanished through the loss of their habitat. Now only those on Niuafo'ou in the Tongan Islands survive. In Samoa the catching of flying birds became a Chiefly sport. In the forest on Tutuila in American Samoa, a star-shaped mound on a hilltop was the ruin of a fort. Many are in fact ancient pigeon-catching grounds, scenes of great competition and skill. Chiefs would appoint catchers renowned for their art. Young pigeons taken from the nest were blinded with birds' claws and then trained to fly to the left or right from a perch while attached to a line of coconut sennit. Adult pigeons were attracted to these expertly flown decoys and, as they fluttered to the centre of the star mound, catchers leapt from their hiding places, armed with huge sweep nets on poles, and scooped them out of the air.

The Pacific Islanders did not always wish to capture animals for food. As their cultures became more complex there was a need to trade goods and to evolve a currency. In Papua New Guinea huge kina shells still decorate the chests of Big Men to signify their wealth. Sperm-whale teeth in Fiji assumed huge value as tambua, the currency of favours between chief, of political alliances, and of lives. Today in the Solomons shell money is still manufactured on Malaita and is traded extensively throughout the islands, principally to purchase wives.

Round chips broken from shells similar to those of oysters are drilled and strung on to lengths of twine, or today of nylon fishing gut. Then they are sanded to necklaces of smooth disc-like beads of white, red and black. Those made entirely from the red rim of the shell have the greatest value, being the most laborious to obtain. As in the case of the stone money of yap, value is attributable according to the time spent in preparation. In the Solomons enormous bundles of white shell money-strings are used to buy a bride: five bundles if she is mediocre, ten if she is a catch.

To Melanesians and Polynesians, red feathers were also of great value for decoration and trade. The magnificent red musk parrots seen in Fiji are also found in Tonga, but they did not get there naturally, they were kidnapped by the Tongans. At the time there was a vibrant trade in the parrots' red feathers, which were used by Fijians to decorate the edges of fine mats for Chiefly occasions. The Tongans also valued them, and used to sail in their double-hulled canoes to Fiji in order to obtain them. some of the parrots were spirited away and released in Tongatapu, the trade in which Fiji had a commanding role in the Pacific was thus undermined. Once they were more widespread in the islands, they survive today only on the ancient island of Eua. The use of red feathers for decoration spread all the way from the Solomons north to Hawaii, and as far east as Tahiti. Small parakeets with red plumage such as Fiji's kula parrot were also popular and traded through the islands. Today these parrots and parakeets have become scarcer and dyed chicken feathers now decorate fine mats.

Further to the west of Fiji, in the Santa Cruz Islands, red feathers carried an even greater value, and were bound into a fascinating story of wealth, spirits, the exchange of wives, and prostitution. The cardinal honey-eater Myzomela cardinalis is widespread in the South pacific, ranging from Samoa to the eastern Solomons, related species also occur in Micronesia. it is smaller than a sparrow but styled like an emperor, the male has black wings and tail, while the rest of its feathers are splashed with scarlet.

An elegant curving black beak allows it to probe the smallest flower, draining it of nectar with a forked tongue as efficient as a drinking straw. Red-feather money is only made on Santa Cruz island by a few specialists whose perceived knowledge of the correct taboos and easily offended spirits that guard the forest traditionally gives them the exclusive right to manufacture currency. First a bird-snearer must fashion small perches covered in sticky latex which he positions in a suitable tree, attaching a nectar-rich flower which is hard to resist or a live bird as decoy. concealing himself behind a blind of palm leaves, he chirps on a special whistle made from a tree bud, so attracting the males to the sticky perch and capturing them.

Most birds die once the red feathers have been plucked from them, but in Hawaii, where magnificent cloaked and helmets were also traditionally made from the red feathers of the abundant honey creepers as well as the highly-prized yellow feathers of much rarer honey-eaters, it as considered a great skill to remove them delicately and release the birds to grow a new set. Menfolk of the Reef and Duff Islands in the eastern Solomons would traditionally sail south, trading their women to Santa Cruz for feather money, which they were themselves unable to make.

The feathers of the cardinal honey-eater were bound into belts up to ten metres long using the plumage of over 300 birds. In the past those women sold as concubines would fetch ten times as much as brides. The women themselves of course, derived no benefit from the trade. concubines lived in the men's meeting house, and the purchaser could purvey them as prostitutes, deriving high income from their services.

Feather money is still used occasionally for trading pigs, or even canoes. Inflation is negligible, because its value declines with age' the colour of the feathers fades even if they are wrapped in leaves and placed near smoky fires, and moths and mould also take their toll. The infiltration of the Australian dollar has, however, undermined the value of feather money. Although there are still few fathers who will marry off their daughters for dollars, the cardinal honey-eater's song is now heard more often in the forest on Santa Cruz

Ade Pearson

The Raining of Early Tahiti
The Original Tahitian: Ancestral Traits B.C.

Life in Tahiti in the mid-eighteenth century was never the unsophisticated paradise of man and nature that it became in romantic European eyes after the raptures of Bougainville. It was instead a far more developed and mature civilization that it has ever been given credit for being. The illusion of primitive, uncorrupted Eden was understandably appealing to disenchanted Europeans in the throes of the Seven Years' War, the conflict that Churchill later called the "real first world war", when England was throwing France out of

America and the struggles in Europe were sowing the seeds of the two great revolutions, American then French, to be followed by the disastrous Napoleonic wars. But Tahitian were not the children their "discoverers so condescendingly characterized them - and as we still are wont to do even after two hundred years.

The arrival of the Polynesians themselves in Tahiti was never recorded in any way that our historians consider valid. It was never incised on clay tablets or penned on scrolls. Instead, it was imprinted, voluminously and meticulously, in the memorized annals of the chiefly families and celebrated in the myths and legends of the race. Such records are little respected, and usually they are even scorned, by our present-day scientific historians. But it is undeniable that these Polynesian people had (and in many ways still have) the most prodigious and detailed memories that are known to exist anywhere in the cultures of mankind.

Their memories are their "documentations", not only in their genealogies which correspond to our history books, but also in their precisely named starry skies (astronomical texts and navigational ephemerides) having individual names for over two hundred stars, and in their incredibly intimate knowledge of the whole scope of their physical surroundings flowers, trees, rocks, fish, birds insects, winds (texts of natural science which had, for instance, separate names for seventy different species of the coconut tree).

So although these people had no written records, their oral ones are marvellously convincing. And Enough was written down by the early missionaries to give us firm though vague outlines of the original happenings and the ensuing events that led to the well-developed Stone Age culture that was thriving in the islands before the white man came to split it into pieces with the iron of his axe and the iron of his creed. Most all other Stone Agers in all parts of the world had graduated slowly over hundreds or even thousands of years - though copper and bronze to iron. The Polynesian transition was a thunderclap of months and a handful of years.

We know now that the racial stocks of the Polynesians set out from southeast Asia some 4000 or 4000 years ago. They migrated through the Indonesian archipelago, where one branch split off southwestward across the Indian Ocean to settle in Madagascar, as the predominant tribes of that fantastically polyglot land, and bestowed three original tongue as the lingua franca of the whole almost continental-size Malgash island. The main group continued to make its way, gradually over centuries of time, past the unfriendly, already inhabited, and malarial-repulsive islands of Melanesia (some think north, some think south of New Guinea), to their first and westernmost island clusters of Fiji, Samoa, and Tonga. They have left along this trail the recently discovered shards of their own highly individualized Lapita pottery. They were quiet people, peaceable, horticultural, and above all maritime - settlers of the littoral, sailors of the high wide seas.

Here these oceanic islanders arrived on virgin land, regrouped and multiplied. Here they developed their deep-sea sailing skills and evolved their great twin-hulled sailing vessels. Here they probably remained for a breathing spell of some five hundred years, while their ancestral Lapita pottery died out. (Gradually they ceased to boil their food in clay vessels and chose instead to bake it in earth ovens, as they still prefer to do today.)

This gradual fading of Lapita pottery from intricate and highly distinctive decorative designs, to plainer and plainer surfaces, to no decoration at all, and then to no pottery at all - is an archaeological mystery (They had no clay of course on the coral atolls, but it was always available on the volcanic islands.) Another mystery is the total absence of the wheel or even, apparently, a knowledge of its principle, not even in boys. They had a disc drill, but this was a reciprocating sort of flywheel, not a burden bearer.

And of course they used rollers to move their great canoes ashore - sometimes indeed they were human bodies. The wheel must have been known in their Asiatic homelands so it too must have faded out like their pottery. But of course virtualy all of their locomotion in the islands was by water. Everywhere they were seaside dwellers and when they made their brief excursions inland into the steep mountains, wheels would have been of little use to them.

After a half millennium in the three western Pacific island clusters, portions of these people set out to the cast to discover new islands. We have radio-carbon dates and artifact sequences that place these migrations at around the time of the birth of Christ.

Many modern scholars believe that it was in these three original island groups, and over this first millennium in the Pacific ocean, that they actually became Polynesian: a conglomerate racial mix, mostly mongoloid, but with some small percentage perhaps of caucasoid, and a dash-in-passing of australoid," developed or evolved what we now recognize as a distinctive Polynesian culture. As population pressures commenced to build up, the more adventurous, or the exiled, or the deprived set sail in migratory waves - waves so small that they probably should be called ripples: eight, ten or a dozen canoe loads in a "fleet," at the most two hundred or three hundred men, women, children, with pigs, dogs, chickens and food plants. At at least one "useless" flower.

It is my personal belief that these adventurers know where they were going, that advance scouting expeditions (of men only, in specially equipped expeditionary canoes) first explored different star-courses as far as what would have been their point of no return, until - probably after several disappointments - they spotted distant new islands. They then sailed back before the prevailing easterly winds to their homelands. With the newly discovered star-courses implanted in the master navigator's brain, they then set about preparing their migratory groups - probably over at least one year, maybe two or even three - so that the star-course they had discovered and chosen could be taken up again, in the proper annual season, to lead them to a new homeland. In such migrations they settled, first off, the central Polynesian islands, the Marquesan and Society groups, some two thousand miles to the east, to the windward of their home islands. Here again, as the archaeological datings tell us, they must have passed a few centuries before reaching the new population densities that would entice or urge or compel them to make exploratory voyages again. To the east they sailed Easter Island. To the south - the Australs and Cooks. To the north - Hawaii. To the southwest - New Zealand. And in the meantime some of them even sailed back to the original western homelands and beyond - the "Outliers."

Thus, they distributed themselves over every inhabitable island to the vast Pacific several hundred years before the Europeans arrived to find them. They had fully populated an oceanic triangle five thousand miles on each side 12 million square miles, an area larger than the whole of Africa, the most widespread single cohesive culture (although one of the smallest in members) anywhere on earth. In so doing, they created - shortly before or after the birth of Christ - a separate civilization of their own, entirely isolated from, and entirely unknown to, the patchwork of civilizations on the other side of the world.

Tahiti Origin

After Polynesia reached its ultimate extent with the colonizations of Eater Island, Hawaii, and New Zealand, each of these two separate civilizations, dating back to the original birthplace in fiji-Tonga-Samoa, had now been going its own way for at least three thousand years - as if both had been on different planets. I have been playing a little geographical-ethnological game comparing events and developments within these two hemispheres, strangers to each other. One, we might call the "hemisphere of land" where men of different races marched or straggled to and fro mixing with each other, warring, trading, interbreeding, emerging as conquerors, subsiding as slaves. The other is the "hemisphere of water," almost equal in area, but minute in living space, where only one race proliferated to all the distant island outposts, retaining its unique homogeneity like a single closely related but widely scattered family. There was almost no intercourse between those outposts. They received variations of stimulus only from variations of ecology, and these, in the tropics, were changes of slight degree.

The comparative highlights of history of these two independent "hemispheres," are shown on the next two following pages. They parallel each other for the three thousand-odd years since their Original Split until the fateful engagement date of A.D. 1767, when the two worlds discovered each other.

Perhaps the best way to convey an impression of what Tahitian life was like in the latter half of the eighteenth century is to contrast some of the basic essentials with our own. Their physical conditions, housing, food, clothing, daily activities, and suchlike have all been detailed so often that they need no repetition here. Of course group comparisons - racial and social - tend to lead to treacherous generalizations, but if they are not used to upgrade or downgrade, they can be interesting to explore. A.G. Keller, disciple of the great William Graham Summer, used to tell his students at Yale, myself among them, that the four fundamental drives of man are Hunger, Love, Vanity, and Fear; in that order.

Let me try to contrast those of the "prehistoric" Polynesian with our own, both contemporary and (since none of us has changed much) present day. Hunger we can in this instance virtually dismiss, because it id nct exist in Polynesia as a constantly motivating forced. To be sure, there were times of sporadic, devastating dryness that caused widespread famine and even impelled migrations, but as we shall se e later, methods of birth control, by abortion and infanticide, seem to have anticipated and ameliorated these aberrational shocks. It is hard for us bread-by-the-swat-of-the-brow people to comprehend this, but everyone, almost all of the time, had plenty of food and experienced no trouble in getting it.

Love is perhaps the most intriguing of the other three drives. The contrasts in the realms of love are subtle and infinitely more complex than the popular assumption. let us start at the beginning. (Conception? No, that belongs later on, in sex.) Birth. Many Polynesian infants never drew a first breath because they were strangled by their parents, usually their fathers, before they could take a first breath. In many respects, though not all, this was the main means of birth control. (Our corresponding one is abortion.)

And birth control was even more important to them on their finite little islands - in an earlier stage of the evolution of their culture - than ours is now in an overpopulated, finite globe. We are only just beginning to realize the absolute necessity of abortion. You may cringe, as the missionaries did, at what they considered the unspeakable horror of infanticide, but if a fetus is to be curtailed, what really is the difference between three months and nine? Mind you, the importance to the Tahitian of a baby's first breath.

If the mother wished to and was able to trick the fetus's father into going fishing or going into the mountains to fetch the orange-coloured plantain, or going to carry a present to his sister on the other side of the island, or whatever, an hour before delivery, so that when he returned the infant was breathing, no power or spirit would make him go through with his obligation to snuff out the life. Because, with the first breath, life had begun m, and no social law told him to be a murderer. His duty to society, and also the mother's to social survival, was to abort the life before it started So let that be the first contrast to our mores.

The next phase of the Love category is probably circumcision, though it may be menstruation. Circumcision was universal. Why this curious and useless operation was practiced throughout that independent oceanic offshoot of the human race is as old and unfathomable a riddle as any worldwide anthropological mystery. The Polynesian's way was a bit different from ours because the foreskin was split only along the top, not ringed round and removed. It was done with the razor-sharp edge of a split bamboo and I think with not much ritual, just a formal family occasion. But it was invariable and oceanwide.

Menstruation was more important - though less, or not at all, ceremonial. The unfortunate maiden was secluded as unclean, untouchable, even unseeable during her menstrual periods. Hers must have been a humiliating ordeal, and it might be said to have lasted a lifetime for a woman. In most ways she was distinctly inferior in Polynesian society. If you ate with a woman you became blind and crippled. The best foods - turtle, pig, and choice portions of others - were forbidden her. No woman was allowed on the community marae, the holy place of worship and sacrifice, although she could participate on the family marae. All of this must stem from the universal prejudice against menstrual blood unclean.

And yet, paradoxically, Polynesian society was in many ways matriarchal. Land was inherited from chiefesses and firstborn females. Lesser chiefs often became greater chiefs through their mother's or wife's lineage, when their father was not so high. The social fabric was shot through with Victorian, big and small. Ariitaimai tells us that no where in the world was marriage a matter of more political and social consequence than in Tahiti. (Ariitaimai will be a significant figure in this narrative. Her Memoirs recounted in Henry Adams toward the end of her life are a wealth of ancient Tahitian lore. We quote her here, long before she was born, because they retell the tales passed down to her through her ancestors, vividly depicting their customs and personalities, and recalling the legends of her race. She herself will be introduced later when, as a young maiden of high birth and dazzling charm, she enters upon her long and subtly influential role in Tahitian history.)

A powerful chiefess was free from her husband's control. She could have as many lovers as she wished but she could not rear a child on non-chiefly origin. He must be killed. There once was a chief of Papara, Ariifaataia, who wanted to marry Maheanu, chiefess of Vaiari and reigning beauty of the island. But she would have none of him. She thought him too ugly so she married a handsome lower born. Maheanu was not disposed to throw her beauty away merely for power. Paradoxes, violent ones, are characteristic of this volatile race. Once these rites or stages of puberty were passed, life was good for nubile Polynesians. They were not only permitted but expected to be promiscuous. Most of them were probably ready for sex before they were teenage, and "experimenting" usually lasted until the early twenties, a matter of eight or ten years. By then perhaps one would know pretty well whom one could marry with some expectation of duration. Captain Bligh enlightens us with a firsthand report.

The women have too great an intercourse with different Men. ... (Yet) it is considered no infidelity, for I have known a Man to have done the Act in the presence of his own Wife, and it is a common thing for the Wife to assist the Husband in these Amours. But what is remarkable, it is not so among those who are not related to one another; it is then a violation if a married Couple err on either side, for if a Man finds another with his Wife he'll kill him if he can, and if the Woman discovers infidelity of the Husband she will certainly take revenge on the Woman.

Inclination seems to be the only binding law of Marriage in this Country, for a Woman will quit her husband if she pleases.

Once married, divorce was rare. Nonmarital sex was all right within reason and discretion, and illegitimate children were gladly adopted, but the family entity was very important, more sacred than personal infatuations or rivalries. After all, and above all, family meant land and inheritance. A man's land, or his wife's land, was his or her future on earth. They never conceived of a future in heaven or hell, just a flapping about of spirits for a while or the enduring virtues of a respected ancestor, represented by his skull stored in the rafters of the house. The constant, permanent symbol, the enduring entity of family was the marae, their open-air, rock-and-coral temple, their only structures of permanence.

We must always keep in mind that these sacred stones were, for the Polynesian, what transcended and made lasting for generations his transient flesh. you might say their maraes were their counterparts of written histories. Ariitaimai says: The marae represented more than all else, the family. Even the god was secondary. The family and the antiquity were alone seriously interesting. ... Genealogy swallowed up history and made law a field of its own, it was the legal code. Let us assume that the next turn of Love is toward children. Here the Polynesian is characteristically more doting and indulgent than the European people. A European's first reaction is that they spoil their babies inordinately. But they also scowl and slap and punish. After a while we realize that the essence of their treatment of children is perhaps more like a game, much play, some of it fun, some of it serious contention and training. Always there is a respect for the child as an equal entity as worthy to be fought with as to be loved. Remember that first breath and that succession on birth. These are embedded things, so long implanted as to become instinctual perhaps. But the enveloping element is attention and care. No Polynesian child is ever neglected.

Following these early-age contrasts between our Love lives and theirs, I would guess there is not much difference in our societal ways. Less divorce, more loyalty to an concern for the older generations, but that is to be expected in a smaller more familial group. Except of course the lifelong inferiority of the female. This is a notable present-day difference but was it two hundred years ago? Women of Europe ate with their men, but the men owned and controlled property to a degree that never was obtained in Polynesia. In France even today the husband owns just about everything.

My great Yale sociologist's third fundamental drive, Vanity, can be very broadly defined to include such urgings or surgings as ambition, artistic attainment, supremacy in sports and war and oratory, heroism and grandeur as well as pride, shame and indulgence. And when so defined there is little basic difference between our social ways, except for the emphasis placed on them. The Polynesian had no money and no interest in it and thus passed by one of our greatest vanities, wealth. Nut the ancient oriental element of "face" was decidedly more important to him than to a European.

His highest art was the art of oratory. He revelled in the prowess of war, but his warfare was much more personal and formalized - more like our jousting of medieval knights. His devotion to sports was, as in ours, an obvious means of displaying personal vanities. wealth. But the ancient oriental element of "face" was decidedly more important to him than to a European. His highest art was the art of oratory. He revelled in the prowess of war, but his warfare was much more personal and formalized - more like our jousting of medieval knights His devotion to sports was, as is ours, an obvious means of displaying personal vanities. But he far exceeded us in diversity.

He played hundreds of games, from childhood up, and played them constantly; stilts, a sort of lob-in-the-air bowling, archery, kite flying, surfboarding, canoe racing of many sorts (first models, then kite sailing, plain sailing, paddling). Such as these were in addition to the usual combative and body-to-body contact or competitive sports like wrestling, racing about and in the water, boxing, etc. But it is notable that boxing was never bloody - body blown only, with the decision resting on a sort of mutual recognition of "points." And we must not forget the never-ceasing "sports" (which we might better call arts) of singing and dancing. Even eating became a refined form of vanity when they competed with each other in huge, recurrent, extravagant feasts.

The spectacular arts of the peripheral Polynesians obviously seem to have sprung from the vanities of their individual creators or their patrons, but these graphic or sculptural arts of the Tahitians are a puzzle, difficult to assess or to compare with those of their fellow Polynesians. The Hawaiians have created the most stunning wooden statutes and the most brilliant use of color in featherwork, the Maori the most intricate and ingenious has relief and screenic carvings, the Easter Islanders the most monumental stone sculpture and the smoothest, most meticulous wooden ancestral figures, the Cook and Austral Islanders exquisite pattern carving and god figures, the Marquesans the most versatile (in all respects) stone and wood carvings and tikis - and in graphics their labyrinthine tatu designs surpass all. Even the relatively stuffy ancestral folks, the Samoans, Tongans, and Fijians, worked wonders with tapa, whale ivory, and shapely wooden tools and implements of war.

In contrast to all of these Polynesian cousins, the Tahitian appears a crude fellow. He has his inspirations. His fly-whisk handles are superb and mysterious, but they do seem frivolous objects on which to lavish one's subtlest craftsmanship. Some authorities think the finest of Tahitian carvings may have been burned in the great bonfires of Christian conversion. But I doubt it. Tahitian gods were sennit-woven bundles, receptacles for the spirits of their gods, never images of them. Their crude stone tikis seem more likely to have been ancestor figures - reminders rather than art. No, the

Tahitian's arts were the living ones: dance, drama, oratory, laughter and fresh-flower dress. In these (whether you call them exhibitionist vanities or performing arts) he rejoiced and excelled, but these arts left no tangible trace for us - only hearsay and echoes, which still reverberate today in the most joyous, playful, life-loving people of the ocean. They had their skills, all right. Their superb canoes bear witness to that. These were were unsurpassed in variety, size, craftsmanship, as well as the art with which they sailed them. And we should emphasize their songs. They were conceived and composed spontaneously, for almost any sort of occasion or occurrence: sad ones for partings, mournful ones for funerals, scornful ones for ridicule, joyous ones for any happy event, and most of all, perhaps, romantic ones for lovers lost or fond, blessed or crossed.

Thus, in the realm of Vanity we might concede to the Tahitians the pleasures and exercises of the body and the senses, and reserve for our own vanities the exhilarations of the intellect and exercises of the brain. So, for the enduring objects of art, one must look around the boarders of Polynesia, not into the center. But for the transitory, lively arts one must turn from the relatively dour, pious, proper, savage, and warlike Hawaiians, Marquesans, Rapans, Rarotongans, Maori, Tongans, and Samoans to the gay, abandoned hedonists of the central core, our Tahitians.

Fear, the last of the four contrasting drives, is for us dominated by fear of loss - poverty, position, health, bodily injury, even loss of mind, insanity. But of course the most pervading and terrorizing of all our fears is death. In studying the Polynesian it has long seemed remarkable to me that of these primary fears of ours none was of much consequence to him. He seems in present reality as well as in historical and prehistorical retrospect to be almost immune to - and certainly casual about - them. One wonders whether instinct can account for this, as it seems persuasively to account for the Polynesian's almost total lack of fear of heights. (Like the American Indian, he can always get a highly paid job walking girders on skyscrapers and bridges.) Is it because he has scampered up coconut trees for untold generations - an acquired characteristic, anathema to geneticists - or was he born that way?

Where there is no pressure of money or lack of food there is obviously no fear of poverty. Position was foreordained by ancestral and parental rank, so there was no losing of it; nor much gaining either. As a race the Polynesians were extraordinarily healthy and had almost no diseases until the white man came: little to worry about on that score. (An exception was elephantiasis, but thought sometimes hideously crippling, it was neither painful nor mortal.) About wounds, broken bones, even cracked skulls, the Polynesian seems to have been philosophical and capable of bearing what we would consider excruciating pain. Nut he knew he would heal quickly (if he didn't die quickly).

Let us set aside for a moment his psychological fears, to consider the Big Fear: earth. Many a learned and experienced, sensitively intuitive writer has reported on the wondrous, calm resignation of the Polynesian confronted with his own death. Most striking are the many reliably recorded instances of people actually willing themselves to dies. They made (and still make) a great fuss about another's death. Never has there been such wailing and lamentation, gashing of foreheads with shark's teeth to let the blood run, chopping off finger joints, setting out corpses to be mummified and watched over, polishing bones and skulls to be hidden away on revered as household companions. Yet, a personal, anticipatory fear of death seems not to have been a significant part of the Polynesian's emotional spectrum. He had no Heaven and no Hell, no afterlife in our sense of the concept (if there is any sense in it). He was fatalistic. he knew his time would come, and everyone who has lived with Polynesians knows that they have only the most casual, offhand sense of time.

But that, on our part, is perhaps a casual, offhand way of dismissing a very complex state of mind or emotion and it leads us back to the bypassed subject of imaginary fears. All people are haunted and harried by ghosts, witches, warlocks, trolls, elves, furies, banshees, and fairies - good and bad. I doubt, however, that they were as manifest and omnipresent or as terrifying in any culture as they were in the Polynesian.

Tahiti Origin

The oromatua and tu'paupau were, and still are, everywhere. These were the ancestral spirits, almost invariably evil. One could hear them in the screech of the night birds, feel them in sudden gusts of wind round the corner, smell them in a crushed tupa crab, taste them in the brimstone of lightning.

The only sense that failed one was sight. They were never to be seen, these evil spirits - even when they ate you or your child or your mother-in-law - remorselessly with long, sharpened teeth. The Polynesian's fear of the spirits of the dead must be classified as psychotic I suppose, because we know it was an imagined fear, and that's the way we classify fears that are not real. Nut they were real to the Polynesian, not the unreal fears that we declare to be those of a sick man. If they were unreal to him, and therefore sink (and therefore curable by a good psychiatrist?), then the whole race was a society of sick men, for the tu'paupaus existed. Everybody knew they did. No one would ever say "Nonsense" or "That's your imagination." They would just hasten to make some magic to scare the evil one away, propitiate him/her, to hide or beg off till tomorrow's morning light. So the Polynesian had his fears all right. It's just that they were different from ours. Might one say his were spiritual and ours are physical? What is Death, spiritual or physical? I hope I have given the reader a glimmer at least of some of the basic contrasts between our separately evolved, ancestral social compositions. I am not advocating Hunger, Love, Vanity, and Fear as in any way being the definitive drives or norms or precepts. No doubt for the present-day social scientist they are now fifty years out of fashion. But this is not intended to be a comprehensive or scientific set of comparisons, merely a sampling. And my old social science teacher's Big Four are certainly with us still.

Two other elements of primary importance is contrasting our two cultures should be added to the

Big Four, climate and religion. Until you have lived for many years in these tropic salt-wind-swept rain-cloud-drenched, sun-scorched, insect-munched islands, it is hard to realize how transient, how rapidly perishable is human flesh and all the fabrications contrived by it. Paintings, books, clothes, houses, even churches of coral blocks disintegrate and melt into the all-embracing compost of these tropics. They dissolve and give up their ghosts at a rate that is astonishing and despairing to those of us who have been building libraries, castles, galleries, cathedrals over the centuries. If, even in our benign temperate climates, our museums are desperately inventing and applying preservatives everywhere, for Florence, Venice, Easter Island and the dissolving Acropolis, how could the Polynesian preserve his precious works?

he didn't: he accepted. He built his house to last at most a generation. His roof he rethatched every four years if woven of nau coco fronds, seven years if of fara pandanus. His canoe hull, which took him two years to hew out, lasted perhaps seven years with constant care; its outrigger two or three years. Everything was contrived, used, discarded. Everything was as expendable, at their slower pace, as plastics, at our frantic pace, are to us today. Everything, that is, except the motor. Not only were its basalt boulders and coral slabs the Tahitian's concept of endurance, but the mana, the magic in them was longer lasting still. for when a clan set forth to found a new settlement on another island, a special stone sacred to that clan, that family, that son, was always taken with them as the founding stone for the new marae, and the name of the ancestral marae was carried on as family names are perpetuated from generation to generation in the descendant marae.

Except perhaps for a brief flirtation with disembodied spirits, I have not touched on the Tahitian's religion. Just where it belongs in these four big categories, I am not sure - perhaps partly in all of them, perhaps mostly in Vanity and Fear. In any case, our religions were of primary importance to both of us in the 1760s and they were different. We will come to that dramatically and poignantly when we come to consider the missionaries, later on. But here we should perhaps sketch a brief outline of the nature of the Polynesian's religion belief. The concept of creation is pithily expressed in the old chant to the originating god:

> *He was there Taaroa . was his name*
> *All about him was emptiness*
> *No where the land . No where the sky*
> *No where the sea . No where man*
> *Taaroa called out . No echo to answer*

> *Then in this solitude he became the world*
> *This knot of roots it is Taaroa*
> *The rocks are he again*
> *Taaroa . The song of the sea*
> *Taaroa . He names himself*
> *Taaroa . Transparence*
> *Taaroa . Eternity*

Taaroa. The Powerful
Creator of the Universe which is but the shell of 'Taaroa Who bestows on it life in beautiful harmony

It is a great pity the Polynesians never evolved a Homer, because their chants and legends are wonderfully rich material, a distinctive as Greek epics, Norse sagas, or Indian Vedas and Puranas. The creation chants tell how Taaroa lay in the darkness of his shell for countless ages. Nothing existed outside this shell - and even the nothingness is specified (no light, no noise, no sea, etc., etc.) at such lengths that the ages do indeed seem boundless. Eventually Taaroa himself becomes weary of inaction and begins to stir. The shell cracks and, at length, he pushes it apart so that its upper half becomes the dome of the sky.

Then he converts the lower portion into the Great foundation Rock, Tumunui, which stands in utter darkness far down in a crevice of the extinct crater of the Temehani, by a great rushing stream of water called Vaitupo. Next, he commences the very long process of manufacturing the other gods, first, Tane (god of forests, rain, fertility), then, the other principals: Tu (stability), Atea (vast expanse). Atea was usually female, and, fertilized by Taaroa, was the begetress of most of the other gods. Oro (war), etc. The list is bounteous and it is also confusing, because in the different island groups (such as the Tuamotus, Cooks, Australs, Hawaii, New Zealand) the various gods were given different attributes and different degrees of importance. (Even Tangaroa, the original, becomes only the god of the sea in Mangaia.) But it is a notable fact that in spite of superficial inconsistencies of function and rank, the same names are used throughout the distant island groups.

The secondary gods set about the housekeeping job of tidying up the universe. They prop up the heavens, create the stars, cover the earth with water, then pull up various islands with a fishing pole and magic hook. Most importantly, one or another of the gods fashions man and woman and sets them to propagating, while still other are clothing the mountains with forests, filling the seas with fish, calling forth all the various winds, and so on. Many of the final tasks, such as fetching fire and fishing up further islands, were left to demigods like Maui, for the members of the Polynesian pantheon, like those of their Greek contemporaries, did a good deal of consorting with humans - in the olden days, that is.

There were many of these demigods. Hiro (patron of thieves) and another Hiro (the master canoe builder), Uahenga (tatu artist), Tafai (the overseas adventurer). But by far the most widely known and most popular of all was Maui, about whom, from the mythologist's point of view, perhaps the most remarkable thing was his ubiquity. Mauitikitiki was his full name, and he is found not only in the folklore of all the Polynesian islands; he was widely known in many areas of Micronesia and Melanesia as well. I believe he is the only hero of primitive religions who covers such distant territories. Thus the Polynesian had a pantheon almost as populous as the Greeks, but the most significant feature of it was that it was clearly man centered, rather than god centered. 'The gods were created for the benefit, though often the chastisement, of man. They had great powers for good and evil, but if one fishing god did not bring good luck or one war god bring victory, even after sacrifices, pleas, praises, and threats, he could be tossed aside and another one enlisted. Tane had been the paramount god for the Tahitians for many generations, but shortly before the white man's arrival (perhaps less than one hundred years before), Oro had come into fashion and power. Through his creation, the Arioi society, Oro's gospel was spreading from Raiatea throughout the islands, and he was certainly in the ascendant when Captain Wallis arrived 1767 on Her Majesty's Ship Dolphin.

Early Face of Tahitian in Humanity - Nature A.D.

On Tahiti in the 1750s and 1760s there was clearly a hierarchical, feudal-like society: of high chiefs, the arii, who were very high indeed; of landowners or nobles, called the raatira; and of an ordinary lowborn class called manahune or teuteu. But unlike his European counterpart even the lowest could feed himself readily and build himself a shelter against the storms. while he lived as a servant-companion in his mater's house or tilled his own "sharecropping" acre of his master's land, he still possessed a very important social right. If he deemed his raatira cruel or excessively demanding or unfair, he could pull up stakes and take his valuable labour to the land of another feudal lord, who would almost certainly welcome him. There were, significantly, no constraints upon this right except, importantly, the consent and sympathy of his fellow manahune.

The house of the highest chief was not much larger or more luxurious than anyone else's. There was no money, no gold, no jewels - and thus no riches piled up. Not even possessions such as mats or bark cloth, houses, or even canoes ever accumulated substantially as one man's property as contrasted with another's. To be sure the high chiefs gathered gifts or tribute in large quantities on occasions, but there were soon redistributed. Nordoff and Hall have a nice way of explaining: In these eastern islands the humblest speaks to the most powerful without any title of respect, with nothing corresponding to our "mister" or "sir." At first one is inclined to believe that here is the beautiful and ideal democracy - the realization of the communist's dream - and there are other things which lead to the same conclusion.

Servants, for one example, are treated with extraordinary consideration and kindliness, when the feast is over the mistress of the household is apt as not to dance with the man who feeds her pigs, or the head of the family to take the arm of the girl who has been waiting on his guests. The truth is that this impression of equality is false; there are not many places in the world where a more rigid social order exists - not of caste, but of classes. In the thousand or fifteen hundred years that they have inhabited the islands the Polynesians have worked out a system of human r3elationships nearer the ultimate, perhaps, than our own idealists would have to believe. Wealth counts for little, birth for everything; it is useless for an islander to think of raising himself in a social way, where he is born he dies, and his children after him.

On the other hand, except for the abstract pleasure of position, there is little to make the small man envious of the great; he eats the same food, his dress is the same, he works as little or as much, and the relation between the two are of the pleasantest. There is a really charming lack of ostentation in these islands, where everything is brown about everyone, and it is useless to pretend to be what one is not. That is oat the root of it al - here is one place in the world, at least, where every man is sure of himself.

The one exception to this general state of relative equality of tangible objects was, however, a very important one. It was land. Land was inherited and land was bequeathed. Its possession was sacred and inviolate to the bloodline of the family that owned it. Such ownership could be enlarged or diminished only by marriage or by death. Even a victorious warrior could not take possession without marrying the widow or sister or daughter of his slain foe; and even then it was not he who took full title, but his progeny by the new wife. Peter Bellwood makes an interesting comment. There was no private ownership of land in the English legal sense, although in practice a lineage or family had the right to use its land in perpetuity.

But though there were high chiefs in Tahiti, there was no king, no supreme monarch or Inca, Emperor, Maharaja or Mikado, as was to be found in virtually all other societies, primitive or sophisticated, all over the world. On this island and indeed on all other Pacific islands and groups of islands, all of them Polynesian, there were balanced clans with chiefs, some stronger or richer in land or prestige than others, but never a supreme chief.

This is a curious societal phenomenon, and I believe you will find it rarely except in the Polynesian race. An American Indian anthropologist might cry, Exception! But the American tribes lived in widely separated, extensive territories, each one speaking its own language, while the Tahitian clans (not tribes) were crowded together on one small island group, with one language only. Each was, in effect, one large family. Tahiti itself had many chiefs of its many districts. These areas were demarcated by the ridges of the many V-shaped valleys that radiate like jagged pieces of a pie from the central mountain peaks of the island.

They vary greatly in size and shape of course, but their boundaries were as precisely known - to the inch - as were the complex kinships of aunts, uncles, cousins, children, and grandchildren of the fundamental owner, male or female. And there are valleys within valleys, which meant chiefs and subchiefs (or taatira) within chiefdoms. There are also islands and peninsulas and other natural divisions and subdivisions. The Polynesian was never a geometrical fellow as far as land was concerned, so in ancestral days there were never plots or blocks of land laid out in surveys as they are so meticulously delineated by the French today. The result was a multitude of landlords and properties that would be impossibly confusing except to a

Polynesian. Fortunately he had a memory and traditions as precise and reliable as a thousand books of affidavits and deeds.

An old-time tale is told of a chief in Raiatea who had a restless and ambitious younger son. Because his older brother was to inherit the land, the younger one set forth in a fine double canoe, well provisioned with fruits, animals, women, and male companions. Four generations lager a descendant of his returned to the valley in Raiatea. There he learned that the original older brother's family had died out, so he claimed the ancient homeland. They asked him for proof of his rights and he recited without flaw the whole genealogy of the family, going back to the originating gods. This would have been a sacred family secret, so he was accepted immediately and granted the chieftainship of the land. Just how so many ranks and files of blood relationships would balance out without a supreme authority is a puzzle to us. But for them it was resolved by a system (can one call such a tangle a "system"?) of clans and chiefs of clans. And in this way, broadly related blood genes took precedence over what might otherwise seem hopelessly scattered and complicated pieces of soil. There were, and had been since time immemorial, four or five or six dominant clans and for many generations preceding the fateful European arrival, these clans had always produced recognized senior, or paramount, chiefs or chiefesses. These were the governing body of the island.

An engaging insight into their personal relationships as well as into the vagaries of Tahitian love is given us by Ariitaimai.

About the year 1650, Tavi was chief of Tautira, and prided himself on being as generous as he was strong. All chiefs were obliged to be generous or they lost the respect and regard of their people, but Tavi was the most generous of all the chiefs of Tahiti. He had a wife,

Taurua of Hatiaa, the most beautiful woman of her time. The chief of Paoara and head of the Tevas at that time was Tuiterai. Like many a vain chief in Tahiti, Tuiterai could not hear of a handsome woman without wanting her, but Tavi's wife was a person of too much consequence to be approached except in the forms of courtesy required between chiefs, and therefore Tuiterai sent his iotai or ambassador to Tavi to request the loan of his wife, with a formal pledge that she should be returned in seven days.

In the Polynesian code of manners, such a request could not be refused without a quarrel. It could not even be evaded without creating ill-feeling that might end in trouble. Had Tuiterai asked for Tavi's child or anything else that he regarded as most precious, the gift would have to be made, subject of course to reciprocity, for every chief was bound to return as good a gift as he received. Tavi did not want to lend his wife, but his pride and perhaps his interest required the sacrifice, and with the best grace he could muster he sent her to Papara. Apparently she made no objection, if the husband was satisfied, the island code had nothing to say to the wife.

Taurua came to Papara, like a Polynesian queen of Sheba, and made her visit to Tuiterai, who immediately fell madly in love with her, showing it by some acts that were amusing, and by others that were too serious for us to laugh at even after eight generations. One of his amusing acts was to take the name Arorua (Aro, breast; rua, two) as a compliment to Taurua's charms and as Tuiterai arorua he is known to this day. The more serious act was that, at the end of the week's visit, he broke his pledge to Tavi, and refused to return Taurua to her husband. This was an outrage of the most grievous kind, such as he might perhaps have inflicted on a very low man - a man fit only for a human sacrifice - built not on a chief; least of all on a chief of equal rank with himself. It was a challenge of force; an act of war. Tuiterai did not attempt to excuse it except on the plea of his infatuation.

No sooner did Tuiterai's refusal reach Tautira than Tavi summond his warriors and sent them against Papara with orders to destroy the land and to kill its chief. Pakpara had no walls like those of Troy to stand a siege, its forces were beaten in battle, Tuiterai was taken, and Taurua was recovered. Among the score of wars fought in early societies about women, and then made the subjects of poetry or legend. The Tahitian variety has a charm of its own because its interest does not end as most of such stories end, with the revenge of the injured party. it should have ended in the usual way, and Tavi had intended to do what any Greek or Norse chief would have done: kill his rival and sack his villages; but the affair took another turn. Tuiterai was wounded, captured, and bound; but when his captors were about to kill him he remonstrated, not with any feeble appeal for mercy, but with the objection, much more forcible to a Polynesian, that a great chief like himself could not be put to death by an inferior. None but an equal could raise his hand against him. None but Tavi must kill Tuiterai.

Tavi's warriors, in spite of their orders, felt the force of the objection, which was, no doubt, in reality an appeal to religious fears, for Tuiterai as head-chief of the Tevas was a person of the most sacred character. They carried him, bound and blindfolded along the shore, some thirty miles, to Tavi. The journey was long, and the wounded chief, feeling his strength fail, urged them on, and as they passed each stream he managed to dip his hand in the water to mark his progress, for he knew the touch of the water in every stream.

When Tavi learned that his warriors had brought Tuiterai alive, he reproached them for disobeying his orders. The pride of generosity had cost him his wife and a war; and still he must forget his character if he put Tuiterai to death with his own hand in his own house. The wars of Tahiti were as cruel and ferocious as the wars of any other early race, but such an act as this would have shocked Tahitian morality and decency. Tavi left himself obliged to spare his rival's life, but between complete vengeance and complete mercy the law knew no interval. A chief spared was a guest and an equal. Tavi gave Tuiterai his life and his freedom and Taurua besides. The legend repeats his words in a song which is still sung as one of the best known Teva ballads.

> *TAVI AND TEURAITERAI*
> *A mau ra i te vahine ai Taurua*
> *Tou hoa ite ee. e matatarai maua e.*
> *Taurua horo poipoi oe iau nei.*
> *To aiai no pohe mai nei au ite ono.*
> *Nau hoi oe i teie nei ra.*
> *A mau ra ia Taurua tou boa ite ee.*
> *Mattarai mauai maua e.*

Take, then, your wife! Taurua! my friend! we are separated, she and I! Taurua, the morning star to me.

For her beauty I would die. You were mine, but now - take, then Taurua! my friend! we are separated, she and I!

nevertheless the overthrow of Papara was too serious a revolution not to affect the politics of the island. Tavi became by his triumph the most powerful chief in all Tahiti, and asserted his power by imposing a rahui. A rahui was a great exercise of authority, which might last a year or more, a sweeping order their everything produced during that time in the whole territory subject to the influence of the chief should be tabu. Not a pig should be killed; not a tapa cloth or fine mat should be made; "not a cock should crow."

The individual mid-eighteenth-century chiefs have come down to us in oral history, as recorded by the early discoverers and missionaries with reputations that can still thrill us today. Prowess in war or physical strength was respected and so was intellectual brilliance - even a master trickster or conniver or thief stood high in the esteem of the community. But the overriding, most worshipful quality of the great leaders was mana: a hard-to-define, commanding combination of wisdom, compassion, firmness, persuasiveness, and understanding - indeed the essence of what are generally recognized as the attributes of greatness in human beings anywhere, anytime. Shortly before the commencement of this narrative, 1750 or so, one chief stood above all in respect, though not necessarily in pow4r.

Vehiatua, like Tavi, was the grand chief of the seaward Teva, the windward section of the most powerful and prestigious of the island's clans. Although Vehiatua was designated chief of the seaward Teva (as contrasted with the landward Teva) this was probably because his residence remained where he was born, in Taiarapu or "Little Tahiti," the peninsular island to the southeast. As their highest chief he was always recognized also by the landward Teva. It was they who owned and controlled the southern or landward districts of the island, Papara and Vaiari (now Papeari), the richest and most desirable lands of all.

During the years preceding its "discovery" by Europe, there were on the island four main chiefs that concern us most. These chiefs were the hui arii, of which the high ones were arii tahi and the highest arii tahi. The whole concept of Tahitian hierachy is complex, and interpretations of it differ depending on who is reporting it, a naval officer, a missionary, a merchant, a native Tahitian. The white man tends to simplify and twist into his own channels; this brown man tends to complicate - to a point of mystification.

The main thing to realize is that power (or persuasion or influence) is rooted in the land or title as well as in the person or in his or her bloodline. Power is also divided into two aspects (1) spiritual power or hereditary prestige, and (2) political power or physical might. Complicate this further with male and female elements of both marriage and blood. Further still with the invariable inheritance of the firstborn was to the chief's title at the very moment of that son's birth, the chief then becoming regent. Multiply by five or six hui arii and their districts, intermarrying, interwarring, drying, and borning. And you have almost as many pieces and places to play with as you would in a chess game.

Another important thing to remember is the extraordinary rights and privileges of a high chief. All must defrock to the waist in his presence. He must be carried on a servant's shoulders everywhere, since whatever land or house or shore is touched by his foot becomes his property forever. He eats only the choicest foods and is usually fed by another. He alone can sit on his marae and wear his red or yellow feather girdle. He alone can command human sacrifice, and so on and on. But all of these sacred honors are strictly limited to his own land and district. The chief of Pakpara is powerless in Paea. He may not even be permitted to visit there without invitation. So in a way our "men" are as move-bound as chessmen. Now, with these distinctions and particulars understood, let us return to the four most interesting chiefs in the Tahiti of the 1760s.

They were (1) Vehiatua of Tautira, who was head of the seaward Teva and by seniority head of both Teva clans, but he was old and sickly and about to die. (2) Amo of Papara, head of the landward Teva and of the richest and most powerful districts of the island, for his authority extended over Vaiari and Mataeia as well - the whole southern section. But Amo was by this time only regent to his young son, Terirere, seven years old in 1769, and his wife was the femme fatale Purea (more of her later). (3) Tuteha chief of the Atehuru, who reigned over the powerful western districts of

Paea and Punaauia and was an uncle of the fourth, last, and most ambitious of the quartet. (4) Tu of Faaa. He was a relatively minor chief compared with the other three, but his clan was the Porionuu in the north, and to its Matavai Bay were about to come Wallis, Cook, Bligh, Vancouver, and the missionaries, bringing with them the powers of firearms and the concepts of kingship that were revolutionary to the Tahitian structure of politics and prestige.

A few years before Wallis's arrival in the dolphin in 1767, Purea, wife of Amo, had ordered the construction o the largest and most spectacular marae in Tahiti shortly after her first extant child was born, about 1762. According to Cook, who measured it carefully but not quite accurately, it was a wonderful piece of Indian Architecture and far exceeds every thing of its kind upon the whole Island, It is a long square of stonework built Pyramidically, the base is 267 feet by 87, the breadth and length at top is 177 feet by 7, it riseth by

Tahiti Origin

large steps all round, like those leading up to a sundial, there are 11 of those each 4 feet high which makes the whole height 44 Feet. Actually Cook's rough calculation must be wrong; it measures 267 by 377 feet, but according to Cook's great biographer, J.C. Beaglehole, it is the greatest in Tahiti and indeed in all of Polynesia, and certainly one of the glories of "Indian Architecture."

Purea's motives in launching this huge enterprise were perhaps to outshine her jealous sisters, to enhance the prestige of Papara, to demonstrate her own power. But mainly the wished to secure the future paramountcy of her son, Terirere. There was also probably mixed into this an urge to rival or even to dominate her powerful husband Amo. Things evidently were not going well between them, for a few years later Amo found other vahines for his sleeping mat, and Purtea was seen with other male companions. Terirere was their only living child, although not the first conceived. They had both been Ariois of the highest order, so no doubt Purea had had a number of previous children that had been disposed of by the conventional infanticide. One suspects that she was anticipating a break with Amo and that this great marae was the best way to insure the future of her son. It was Teriirere's marae; not even his father, Amo, could sit in the place of honor. Sometime previously Terii had been invested with the sacred and feather girdle of Papara.

The story is an involved one. Purea was not the eldest, but she came from a sizable family of sons and daughters of a very high chief. The older sisters resented the arrogance and pride and ambition of the younger one. They were also no doubt jealous of her radiant charm, for Purea was evidently blessed by the gods, she outshone even the great Amo. And she has always seemed to get her willful way - to wind up successfully in spite of her imperious airs. But this time she went too far. One of her sisters-in-law was refused the hospitalities and rights due her rank. The child of another was insulted. A local war broke out. Mighty Papara was overwhelmed. Amo and Purea took to the mountains and another chiefly balance had been upset. All this had occurred before the coming of the white man, but by then the situation had been resolved. Purea was back to greet Wallis and enough in her old spirits so that he dubbed her queen of all Tahiti. But the upheaval had left an uncertainty in the air and enough disequilibrium amount the older, higher chiefs so that a younger and lesser one could make progress - with European arms - a challenge that would never have been permitted had the old order been stable at the time.

Ariitamai (our heroine Huruata Salmon) told Henry Adams, in her old age and looking back on those days of her native Papara's glory and disaster, that it was usually a female who wrecked a kingdom, and as long as her beloved Papara was fated to be humbled she was glad that at least her Great-Aunt Purea was a surpassingly beautiful woman. Pura was the "Oberea" of Samuel Wallis, first European discover of Tahiti. In his eyes she was Queen of the island, a glamorous lady who arrived in a "royal barge," a large double canoe with a spacious deck-house where she and her "ladies-in-waiting" disported themselves, feasted, and entertained. Ashore, he tells us, she had a house 327 feet long, 42 feet wide, and 30 feet high (but actually it was the district council house, not Oberea's private manse). Wallis apparently thought that she had fallen in love with him and one suspects that if he had not been so ill a royal romance of sorts might have come about. he was a prime novelty, the first great white chief, and besides, by this time Amo was casting elsewhere.

Purea's affair with the Dolpin's captain, if you can call it that, was brief and fleeting, but she is for us a convenient traditional personage. She figures importantly just a few years later in Cook's introduction to "La Nouvelle Cythere."

First Contact with the Explorers

1767 et seq.

Something very strange was brewing in Europe at this time. For centuries past there had been massive marchings of peoples in the hemisphere of land, unknown of course to the people of the ocean. Aryan hordes had poured from Persia to India between 2000 and 1200 B.C. Later Alexander had led the Greeks to India through Asia Minor. The Mongol hordes under Genghis Khan overran China. Greatest of all was the methodical Roman conquest of the Mediterranean basin, lasting some one thousand years until Attila the

Hun and the Visigoth raiders toppled its tired, degenerate civilization. Then, after those visit continental upheavals, came the thousand-year Medieval slumber, during the same years when the Polynesians were regrouping and evolving themselves in the hemisphere of water on the western approaches to the Pacific.

The land masses of Eurasia and of Africa north of the Sahara were all spoken for now. In India and china, the two massive civilizations of Asia had long ago filled to overflowing their huge ecological niches. By the 1450s the restless and aggressive peoples of the European and Middle Eastern earth had reached the ultimate barriers of the world as they conceived its finite extent, a land mass encompassed by a mysterious infinite sea. Then Columbus found a new world and each nation suddenly realized - as the Polynesians had before them on the other side of the globe - that the sea, instead of the fearsome barrier it had always been, was instead a highroad to new worlds to conquer. All that was needed were ships, and one by one the competitive states of Europe began to build them. Then the whole European subcontinent began to burst forth, not as a massive entity but in successive national pulsations. And these new ventures were selective invasions by sea in ships over the oceans, in place of the massive footslogging invasions of past history. Curiously enough this was roughly the same time when the Polynesians were reaching by sea their ultimate population limits on their most recently settled peripheral islands.

Of course ships had been known long time since in Europe, but until Columbus, Europeans had never crossed the oceans. They had been coastal sailors only, not deep-water men. An exception was the Norsemen venturing to Greenland, island-hopping by way of the Shetlands, Faeroes, and Iceland, and even touching North America. But those open-water stretches were no more than three in four hundred miles. No one paid much attention to these Norsemen and purposely they did not spread the news of their sporadic feats.

European maritime historians boast of the Phoenicians within the "vast' Mediterranean and of voyages out of the Strait of Gibraltar and along the Atlantic coasts to fetch lead and tin from Cornwall and Ireland. Arab dhows even sailed eastward to India, probably north-coasting the Arabian Sea. These were brave deeds, from Ulysses onward, but they were eventually coastal, rarely more than a few days out of sight of land. Even the Azores and Canaries wee probably not discovered or at least not settled, until the twelfth or thirteenth century, more than one thousand years after the Polynesians were crossing the dark blue Pacific.

Only the ancestors of our Polynesians could claim true deep-sea voyaging before Columbus. And strangely enough, these illiterate "primitives" achieved not only that precedence but voyages of well over two thousand miles of open ocean. Nobody paid attention to them either. Indeed nobody in Europe even knew there was an ocean over there beyond the comfortable earthy borders of their non globular., flat, fearsomely water-surrounded world. The Polynesian concept was another story in another separate world, equally flat in projection, but a world of friendly water punctuated by rich little islands and similarly surrounded by the forbidding unknown.

Following the Portuguese pioneers, the Spaniards were of course the first conquistadores and they quickly gobbled up the enormous tropical areas of the new continents all the way from Florida in California southward to Peru. What a conquest! Larger than the whole of Europe and North Africa combines, indeed just about the same size as the whole of Europe's then known world except for hazy Asia, and the African deserts and jungles. No wonder such huge tracts made them greedy for more, and when the easy gold ran thin, no wonder they reached out over the barren North Pacific to the Philippines and the lands of spice. No wonder also that these Spaniards soon began to run thin themselves, and in time were the first to lose the only thing they eve really wanted: overseas gold.

Next came the Dutchmen to the East Indies and so entranced were they with the immediate riches of spices and trade that they ignored the austral continent which they had discovered and could have exploit4ed for their exploding population. It was left then to the English and the French to conquer the rest of the world and we must give them some credit for they went out not exclusively to exploit but also to settle and, as they thought, to improve. Not too much credit, because they did some long-term exploiting also, especially in India, Egypt, Indo-china, Algeria. Their Pacific settlements were dumpings, at first, of excess and unwanted growths in their own populations: criminals first, to empty their prisons into penal colonies, then nonconformists, religious fanatics, splinter sects - undesirables who were too respectable intellectually to be classed as lawbreakers, yet clearly citizens to be got rid of. Things at home were made difficult enough for these people so that most of them shipped themselves off to North America, Australia and New Zealand. Alas, they were self-righteous enough to decimate indigenous populations without a qualm: American Indians and Australian Aborigines, New Zealand Maori.

The English were a bit better at it than their rivals the French because, although the two countries whacked up the remaining world between them, the English bested the French in the long run because Englishmen came to stay, to work, to become Americans and Australians. Frenchmen came to suffer a necessary separation from La Belle France, always harboring within them a craving to return home again. They had not their hearts in it as did the English, and so, in time, they were thrown out, expelled militantly from America, thwarted in New Zealand, contained in the Middle East, excluded from India and southern Africa. So the whole world was carved up as Europe helped herself while Russia slept and china's inner kingdom suffered humiliating intrusions even though she retained the basic integrity that she is at last asserting today. Japan fended off fiercely all attempts even of contrast, but of course there was not much to conquer in those overpopulated, resource-poor islands.

The rest of the world submitted, surly bit subservient, as their peoples had always been, to remote masters. Whether the conquerors were white or black or yellow, Muslim, Christian, Buddhist, Confucian, or Hindu made little difference. Exploitation was the rule of the centuries. All stay-at-home peoples of the land half of the word were born and bred to it. A Release from bondage was to come eventually in this twentieth century from their English masters, through the consciences and the weaknesses of their local governors powered by the gradual, oh-so-slow emergence of the concept of the equality of man. And the English example was, in time, to se that whole world tumultuously, bloodily, unpeacefully free.

But not the Pacific water world, not yet. And Tahiti? Here in microcosm was, and still is, a test-tube study of the evils and dubious blessings of the implacable Anglo-French drive to colonial conquest. North America had been staked out for the English when Wolfe defeated Montcalm at Quebec in 1759. And, oddly enough these men participated in this critical battle who were later to loom large on Tahiti's horizon: Samuel Wallis, a midshipman transporting troops for Wolfe, Louis de Bougainville, then a soldier, aide-de-camp to Montcalm; and James Cook, a promising young marine surveyor in the Royal Navy who charted the river approaches for the British army landings.

The American Revolution had little direct effect on Tahiti except that it is interesting to note that Cook's voyages of exploration were protected from harassment by an *understanding of mutual agreement between the British and their warring American colonies. In March 1779, Benjamin Franklin, then American ambassador to France, issued from his residence of Passy an open letter to all American shipmasters, bidding them aid Captain Cook's ships, despite their nationality, designating his mission an undertaking truly laudable in itself, as the increase of geographical knowledge facilitates the communication between distant nations, in the exchange of useful products and manufactures, and the extension of arts, whereby the common enjoyments of human life are multiplied and augmented in general. ...* A noble gesture even though the Congress failed to support it.

The French Revolution distracted both English and French from their colonizing ambitions for some decades while Nelson, heroically, and Napoleon, humiliatingly, were being disposed of. The British, having won the battle of Trafalgar in 1805, got a splendid head start at sea while the French were recovering from their gigantic European and domestic landward upheavals. The English secured the continent of Australia with ease, but they beat their rivals to the prize colonizing potential of New Zealand by only a few months.

A French expedition under Lavaud, who was later to become the second governor of Tahiti, had se tout to take over New Zealand early in 1840 and arrived at the Bay of Islands in May to find the British already in possession and to learn that the infamous Treaty of Waitangi had been signed only thirteen days before Lavaud had set sail from Brest. The French made a pass at the South Island, but after a bit of skirmishing, the local British commander was able to bluff them out of this alternative prize.

Now this digression to New Zealand may seem incidental to a history of Tahiti, but I feel it has a significant bearing because, as a result of their success in the western Pacific, the British were apparently willing to concede the Marquesas Islands and Tahiti to the French as consolation prizes. The scattered island world was there for the taking. As you read of protest and riposte, of give and take, of national prides inflamed and national tempers soothed in the minutes and demarches, the speeches and rhetoric that flew back and forth across the Channel from the British Foreign Office to the Ministry of State, even from the Chamber of Deputies to the House of Commons, you realize that a military and diplomatic game of chess was being played between these old rivals who at that time certainly considered themselves, and were indeed generally recognized as, the two great superpowers of the earth.

A couple of pawns like Tahiti and the Marquesas could readily be sacrificed for a rook like new Zealand. And even a knight such as New Caledonia could b4e conceded for another pawn such as Norfolk while Fiji, the Solomons, the New Hebrides, and others awaited their turns. A concrete expression of this state of affairs appears in the instructions issued to Bougainville where Choiseul said that France would spare no pains to gain a footing also, in whatever seas the English attempt to settle in; she would never consent to the formation by England of new colonies in anyh part of the world unless she herself were free to form colonies in like manner. Of course an Englishman at the time would have discounted this as blustering French amour propre, but England was having trouble with her American colonies and did not want to add to her martial commitments for the sake of a few romantic islands.

Tahiti Origin

This of course is to speak only of the Pacific: far-flung, small-fry compared to North Africa, where France was straining for Algeria and England for Egypt and both of them for the Middle East, India, Indochina, and such sub-Saharan lands as the Cape provinces and Madagascar. But before the guns began to talk, the forces of the Gospels had begun to be deployed. The Spaniards had of course blazed the trails in reverse of the order to come, sending their priests into the wreckage left by their soldiers of the Aztec and Inca civilizations to consolidate their power so that their gold miners and merchants could reap the long-term rewards of conquest. The stakes were different in the Pacific: no gold mines or plantations, only islands - but such beautiful smiling islands with such peaceful smiling people on them. First off they seemed best for penal colonies, then for settlers, and always for strategic military bastions or supply depots on the great trade routes to China. here again on the spiritual battlefield the British heat their rivals to the draw. The London Missionary Society sent out its first "troops" in 1797 and gained a foothold in Tahiti that ;makes Protestantism dominant to this day in spite of official French roman Catholic rule.

But we are getting ahead of ourselves. Before considering such post-contact occurrences, let us review briefly the men and events that brought the Europeans to Tahiti and in so doing revolutionized its way of life and began the ravishment of its long-established culture. The first to arrive was that same Samuel Wallis, midshipman, landing troops on the Plains of Abraham. Now in 1767 he is a Lieutenant in the British Navy in command of H.M.S. Dolphin on a voyage of exploration to find the fabulous southern continent that, as all the great European geographers agreed, must be spread across the antipodes to balance the known land masses of the Northern hemisphere. Mind you, the popular recognition of the roundness of the globe and especially the immensity of its size were relatively new concepts to the European mind. Columbus's voyages had led to the discovery of the two huge new continents. Magellan had spanned the North Pacific and revealed its stunning extent. surely, thought the sages of the Royal Society and My Lords of the Admiralty, there must lie a vast new continent in the vast new Southern Ocean. What an exciting idea and nothing to gainsay it.

But Samuel Wallis did not find it. He was a poor choice for the job. He arrived at Tahiti sick and discouraged after a fearful battle with the elements to negotiate the Southern Straits. Tahiti's natives seemed friendly at first, but they soon attacked with torrents of slingstones from their canoes. Wallis retaliated with musket fire, grapeshot and cannon ball, killing and wounding dozens of the astounded and helpless islanders. when they had fled to the hills, he sent his men ashore to destroy wantonly their beached canoes

- beautiful craft, the most precious fruit of hundreds of man-years of patient Tahitian labor and skill.

This was to teach them a lesson. They learned it well, this first, swift, brutal revelation of the cruel power and implacable nature of their white visitors. After that there was no more lethal hostility, only the age-old Polynesian games of thievery and seduction. To protect his men, Wallis set a line of defense along the little river that ran between the mainland and the point where his scurvy-ridden crew was recuperating.

His armed patrols were effective enough in keeping the Tahitians safely to their side of the stream, but he had not reckoned on the beguiling wiles of the provocative vahines and soon found that most of his ailing invalids were crossing over to infiltrate the palms and bushes Pursuits, threats, disciplines, rewards - no counter-measures that Wallis could muster were equal to the attractions of the wenches, so he soon pulled up anchor and, after only five weeks in port, almost all of which he himself spent on board ship, he sailed out of lovely Matavai Bay. The visit must have had a peculiar effect on his mind, for instead of heading south to pursue the designated purpose of his secret exploratory mission, he headed north and then west to encounter only a few tiny islands before engaging the conventional homeward route of the China trade.

Wallis himself kept a careful journal as he was required to do by Royal Navy orders. But it is dull reading and has never been published. His sailing master however, one George Robertson, has left us many, pithy human insights.

The country hade the most Beautiful appearance its posable to Imagin, from the shore side, one two and three miles Back their is a fine Leavel country that appears to be all laid out in plantations, and the regular built Houses seems to be without number, all allong the Coast, they appeared lyke long farmers Barns and seemed to be all very neatly thatched, with Great Numbers of Cocoa Nut Trees and several oyr trees that we could not know the name of all allong the shore - the Interior part of the country is very Mountainous but their is beautiful valeys between the Mountains - from the foot of the Mountains half way up the Country appears to be all fine pasture land, except a few places which seemed to be plowed or dug up for planting or sowing some sort of seed-from that to the very topes of the mountains is all full of tall trees but what sort they are I know not but the whole was Green. This appears to be the most populoss country I ever saw, the whole shore side was lined with men, women and children all the way we Saild along.

the natives ... brought o the water side a good many fine young Girls down of different colours, some was a light coper collour oyrs a mullato and some almost if not altogether White - this new sight Attract our mens fance a good dale, and the natives observd it, and made the young girls play a great many droll wanting (wanton) tricks, and the men made signs of friendship to entice our people ashoar, but they prudently referd going ashore, untill we were better aquanted with the temper of this people.

Their love of Iron is so great that the women (or rather Girls, for they were very young and small) prostitute themselves to any of our People for a Nail, hardly looking upon Knives, Beads, or any toy. Yet I must say yt the Girls who were of the white sort would admit of any Freedom but the last ... the Young Girls ... had now rose their price ... from a twenty to a thirty penny nail, to a forty penny nail, and some was so extravagant as to demand a Seven or nine inch Spick.

What must the Tahitian have thought of this sudden while-skinned, womanless arrival? He had known for generations a mythical tale of a white god arriving in a single-hull canoe - a vessel that would have been inconceivable to him except in a dream. Would he have accepted this miraculous presence from another world as Europe accepted the discovery of Columbus? Probably. No one there knew of the finite contours of our globe. No one had thought to sail out into ultra-oceanic space. for three thousand years these people had had their own self-contained world and one senses, perhaps irrationally but somehow intuitively, that they were getting tired of it. Ready to find something fresh and new and bigger, as we are today ready for the discovery of outer space. As we look back on these islanders, they were wonderfully adaptable and long accustomed to change of all sorts. Our advent did not appear to shatter them, though actually it did. They had long been accustomed to changing names: important ones of high chiefs because of a sneeze in the night; of their staff of life, breadfruit, from uru to maiore because a bad chief chose to make his name Uru.

Captain Bligh obliges us again with an on-the-scene comment: *The People here as well as in England have several Names, and being differently used, it is frequently perplexing when the same person is spoke of, to know who is meant. Every Chief has perhaps a dozen Names in the course of 30 Years, so the Man or woman that has been spoken of by one Navigator under a particular name, will not be known by another, unless other causes lead to a Discovery.... I now find that Otoo or more properly Tynah, for that is his name since the Sovereignty is devolved to his son, is still the greatest personage on this part of the Island. I shall now therefore for the future call him Tynah, the name of Otoo or Too, as it is differently spoken, being now the name of his eldest Son who is between five and Six years Old, reigning under the direction of his Father, whose name always goes from him as soon as he has a*

Son. Under such circumstances that a Parent should lose his power and authority is a most extraordinary thing, but I believe it is not less true, than it is unnatural and absurd.

Even changes of gods took place; such as the peaceful Tane of love and plenty to the warrior Oro, eater of men. Eventually they tossed aside their ancient religion and embraced the new one. It took some years and much agony to do so, but they had apparently reached a stage when the old religion was flagging. Perhaps they were bored with Oro and their many minor gods and ready for a fresh new world.

The next European to land on our island was Count Louis Antoine de Bougainville whom we first noted in the siege and capture of Quebec as a aide-de-camp of the glamorous French Commander Montcalm. Bougainville had come a long way in the ensuing decade. An offspring of a middle-class but well-funded and influential family, he had soon shown an unusual intelligence and charm of personality. he had proved himself a bright and energetic aide to the general. His army was ready to send him swiftly upward, but he was evidently more interested in science, the arts, adventure, society, and diplomacy than in military tactics or strategy. he went to London to study and soon became a member of the royal Society, a rare and distinguished compliment for a young French soldier-diplomat who was not of noble blood. Then somehow he made friends in Paris in the powerful Ministry of the Marine and became a sailor, later an admiral no less, and was now in charge of the first of a series of resplendent voyages of discovery to be sent out and welcomed back with all the trimmings by His Royal Majesty Louis XV, king of the French.

He had set sail from France in 1766 before Wallis had returned to Europe with the news of the discovery of Tahiti, so his own discovery in 1768 was a genuine one in the European, though not of course in the Polynesian, sense. He landed on the east coast of the island and nearly lost his two ships in a meager, exposed harbor, thereby showing he was not much of a sailor, for he could easily have coasted to protected harbors on the lee side. He was not much of an explorer either, in spite of the paeans of French historians, for he stayed only eight or nine days and walked hardly a mile from his ship. It would indeed seem to have been an uneventful and unimaginative visit. and yet it inspired the most romantic reaction of any discovery in history. Imagine yourself a European of those times.

Columbus had only recently (two hundred fifty years was a short interval then) revealed the existence of two huge, utterly new continents. You had just begun to realize the immensity of the Pacific. Of course there must be a whole new continent to find and of course these new islands and new lands would be peopled with Jean-Jacques Rousseau's untouched, unspoiled children of nature - a living laboratory to make the dreams of the master philosopher and his thousands of cultists throughout Europe emerge from romantic idealism into suddenly confirming physical reality.

Bougainville named his island "La Nouvelle Cythere" after the legendary birthplace of Aphrodite and described its inhabitants as such happy children of a South Sea Eden that a whole newly strengthened mythology of the virtues of Man in Nature swept the cynical civilized world of the day. Indeed it still nourishes many a fond and foolish dreamer. Although Bougainville protested that his reports had been overblown, he did bring back with him a comely Tahitian lad who almost instantly took the fickle social world of Paris by storm. Ahutoru with his Polynesian smiles, courtesies and, perhaps, his Polynesian prowess in ladies' boudoirs, was Exhibit A in the flesh, the Man of Nature par excellence. Bougainville also leaves us a telling insight into the intimate ways of Polynesian humanity and, coming from an intellectual Frenchman, it is naturally a bit more sophisticated, though perhaps no more intuitively unerring, than the perceptions of George Robertson.

Polygamy seems established amongst them, at least it is so amongst the chief people. As love is their only passion, the great number of women is the only luxury of the opulent. Their children are taken care of, both by their fathers and their mothers. It is not the custom at Tahiti, that the men occupied only with their fishery and their wars, leave to the weaker sex the toilsome works of husbandry and agriculture. Here a gentle indolence falls to the shore of the women; and the endeavors to please are their most serious occupation. I cannot say whether their marriage is a civil contract, or whether it is consecrated by religion, whether it is indissoluble, or subject to the laws of divorce. Be this as it will, the wives owe their husbands a blind submission, they would wash with their blood any infidelity committed without their husband's consent. That, it is true, is easily obtained, and jealousy is so unknown a passion here, that the husband is commonly the first who persuades his wife to yield to another.

An unmarried women suffers no constraint on that account; every thing invited her to follow the inclination of her heart, or the instinct of her sensuality; and public applause honours her defeat: nor does it appear, that how great soever the number of her previous lovers may have been, it should prove an obstacle to her meting with a husband afterwards. Then wherefore should she resist the influence of the climate, or the seduction of examples: the very air which people breathe, their songs, their dances, almost constantly attended within decent postures, all conspire to call to mind the sweets of love, all engage to give themselves up to them. They dance to the sound of a kind of drum, and when they sing, they accompany their voices with a very soft kind of flute, with three or four holes, which, as I have observed above, the blow with their noses. They likewise practice a kind of wrestling; which, at the same time, is both exercise and play to them, of wrestling; which, at the same time, is both exercise and play to them.

Thus accustomed to live continually immersed in pleasure the people of Tahiti have acquired a witty and humorous temper, which is the offspring of ease and Joy.

How did he learn so much in so short a time? Another incident of Bougainville's brief dalliance is an amusing contrast to the two far-distant cultures. Philbert de Commerson, who was the surgeon and naturalist on Bougainville's companion ship, the Etoile, had brought with him a young valet to tend his personal needs and to help him with his collections, sketches, and records. When the valet first went ashore on an errand for his master, the Tahitians promptly laid hands on him and playfully stripped off his clothing, thereby revealing to his astonished shipmates an indubitable young maiden, one Jeanne Baret, who went on to become the first female of Homo sapiens (or perhaps any other species) to circumnavigate the globe.

Next the course and by far the most importantly comes our final member of the trio of Quebec, James Cook, to observe the transit of Venus in 1769 and on his second voyage in 1772-75 to zigzag through the southern reaches of the ocean and prove at last that there was no such thing as a great earth-balancing southern continent. His accomplishments as an explorer are too well known to need review here and he was not a particularly sensitive observer and recorder of Polynesian life, but there are a couple of entries in his journal that reintroduce to us Ariitaimai's Great-Aunt Purea, the one who had caused such trouble in Papara. she was in her forties now, well past her prime. In the words of Cook's young astronomer William Wales, an old demi-rip of quality.

Tuesday June 20th, 1769. Last night Obarea (Purea) made us a Viset who we have not seen for some time we were told of her coming and that she would bring with her some of the Stolen things, which we gave credit to because we knew several of them were in her possession, but we were surprised to find this woman put her self wholy in our power and not bring with her one article of what we had lost. The excuse she made was that her gallant, a Man that used to be along with her, did steal them and she had beat him and turn'd him away; but she was so sensible of her own guilt that she was ready to drop down through fear -- and yet she had resolution enough to insist upon sleeping in Mr Bank's Tent all night and was with difficulty prevailed upon to go to her Canoe altho no one took the least notice at her.

Tahiti Origin

In the Morning she brought her Canoe with every thing she had to the Gate of the Fort, after which we could not help admiring her for her Courage and the confidence she seem'd to place in us and thought that we could do no less than to receive her into favour and accept the presents she had brought us which Consisted of a Hog a Dog some Bread fruit & Plantains. We refused to except of the Dog as being an animal we had no use for, at which she seem'd a little surprized and told us that it was very good eating and we very soon had an opportunity to find that it was so, for Mr Banks having brought a basket of fruit in which happened to be the thigh of a Dog dress'd, of this several of us taisted and found that it was meat not to be despise'd and therefore took Obarea's dog and had him immidiately dress'd by some of the Natives in the following manner.

They first mad a fire, and heated some small Stones, while this was doing the Dog was Strangle'd and the hair got off by laying him frequently upon the fire, and as clean as if it had been scalded off with hot water, his entrails were taken out and the whole washed clean, and as soon as the stones and hole was sufficiently heated, the fire was put out, and part of the Stones were left in the bottom of the hole, upon these stones were laid Green leaves and upon them the Dog together with the entrails. These were likewise cover'd with leaves and over them hot stones, and then the whole was close cover'd with mould: after he had laid there about 4 hours, the Oven (for so I must call it) was open'd and the Dog taken out whole and well done, and it was the opinion of every one who taisted of it that they Never eat sweeter meat, we therefore resolved for the future not to despise Dog flesh. It is in this manner that the Natives dress, or Bake all their Victuals that require it, Flesh, Fish and fruit.

Wednesday 21st. This morning a chief whose name is Oamo (Amo) and one we had not seen before, came to the fort, there came with him a Boy about 7 years of Age and a young woman about 18 or 20, at the time of their coming Obarea and several others were in the fort, they sent out to meet them, having first uncover'd their heads and bodies as low as their waists and the same thing was done by all those that were on the out side of the fort, as we looked upon this as a ceremonial Respect and had not seen it paid to any one before we thought that this Oamo must be some extraordinary person, and wonder'd to see so little notice taken of him after the Ceremony was over.

The young woman that came along with him could not be preva'ld upon to come into the fort and the boy was carried upon a Mans Back, altho he was as able to walk as the Man who carried him. This lead us to inquire who they were and we was inform'd that the Boy was Heir apparent to the Sovereignty of the Island and the young woman was his sister and as such the respect was paid them, which was due to no one else except the Areedehi which was not Tootaha from what we could learn, but some other person who we had not seen, or like to do, for they say that he is no friend of ours and therefore will not come near us. The young boy above mentioned is Son of Oamo by Obarea, but Oamo and Obarea did not at this time live together as man and wife he not being able to endure with her troublesome disposission, I mention this because it shows that separation in the Marriage state is not unknown to this people.

But Cook's significance to future internal events in the island lay not in his splendid explorations and discoveries, but in his fixation on Matavai Bay as the best of anchorages and his bequest of it to future English mariners. He thus inadvertently allied European power with the weaker, traditionally inferior chiefs of the north and opened the way for the overthrow of the political equilibrium of the ancient Tahitian culture. Other explorers to these islands and the Marwquesas followed the cautious and methodical Vancouver, the Russians Lisiansky and Kotzebue, the Americans Porter and Ingraham.

More were to follow at intervals well into the 1800s. But the most notable reporter of our chief interest here, the human natures of the island people, was cook's sailing master on his third and final voyage, William Bligh. Bligh is of course best known for the mutiny, for its complex initial causes for Bligh's heroic escape, and for the dramatic fate of the mutineers on Pitcairn Island. Little notice has been taken, however, of the serious effects on the Tahitians caused by the presence of the desperadoes who remained on the island for nearly two turbulent and corrupting years before their recapture by the British authorities (but more of that later).

And Bligh should be given credit for being one of the keenest observers of the idiosyncracies of these strangely individualistic beings, whom he so acutely perceived as humans while most other of Her Majesty's officers were looking down their noses at them as heathens, savages, or at best children. I have sprinkled his comments through the test and will sum up with: I was under the necessity this afternoon to punish Alexn. Smith with 12 lashes for suffering the Gudgeon of the large Cutter to be drawn out without knowing it. Several chiefs were on board at the time, and with their Wives interceded for the Man, but seeing it had no effect they retired, and the women in general showed every degree of Sympathy which marked them to be the most humane and affectionate creatures in the World.

After the early explorers come the first of the aforementioned missionaries in the good ship duff in 1797. Then the infiltrators - deserters, traders, beachcombers, merchants. After them the whalers, having pretty much fished out the Atlantic, break into our ocean and, finding Tahiti the best place to rest and refresh and regale themselves, bring as many as seventy or eighty ships a year into Papeete in the late 1830s. Their apostle is Herman Melville in 1843, but again we are getting ahead of our story.

The Missionaries, 1797

The missionaries were a curious breed. The London Missionary Society was founded in 1795, its moving and guiding spirit a Reverend Thomas Haweis. The founders and directors were a group of middle-class zealots apparently quite different from the aristocrats of the Church of England. They came from a variety of sects. Methodists, Baptists, Calvanists, Wesleyans, Presbyterians, rebels one might say, or escapists from the Established Anglican Church. Many such religious renegades had been migrating to the American colonies starting, of course, with the Mayflower. There they had continued their boisterous rebelliousness among themselves, Roger Williams splintering off to Rhode Island, a mass exodus to New Jersey, Cotton Mather and Jonathan Edwards fulminating from their pulpits, Salem burning its witches and so on for nearly a century.

But now, after the revolution, America was no longer a brace of colonies, so where could the English nonconformist go? Fortunately new worlds had just been found by the explorers and they were filled with savages who had never heard of the True God and were reveling in heathen orgies that were pouring vast quantities of souls into Satan's lap as he sat smiling in Hell. These misguided children of nature knew nothing, alas, of their original sin. No one had told them about Adam and Eve and the Apple. So the confident saviors of London banded together, raised money from pious widows and alms-begging children; raised recruits partly from their own ordained brethren, but mostly from artisans, mechanics, carpenters ....

Turmoil: the Old Order Changes - 1815

Meanwhile the social structure of Tahiti was changing considerably. The traditional order of four or five more-or-less equal high chiefs had been upset by European monarchical tradition, by European arms and by the driving ambitions of one relatively low-ranking but ruthless line of chiefs who saw and seized their chance to become English-type "kings" with the help of muskets from English explorers and traders and even from English missionaries needing to protect themselves. A chief of "Tuamotuan ancestry named Tu, who later renamed himself Pomare (and still later his son, Pomare II) became for the first time in its history the supreme chief of all Tahiti, introducing dictatorship to what had been an essentially democratic society.

The Pomares' ancestral lands were the low-lying coral atolls to the northeast. They are a huge archipelago some six hundred miles from end to end composed of nearly a hundred scattered islands, the remnants of what must have been a huge mountain range many, many millions of years ago. The tectonic plate on which these volcanoes rested had long since subsided into the Pacific floor, leaving rings of coral on the surface that had grown upward with the sun as their foundations sank. They were inhabited by a fierce branch of Polynesian warriors who were feared and despised by their neighbors to the northeast in the high, mountainous Marquesas Islands and their opposite neighbors to the southwest in the Society Islands.

The Tuamotuans were a hardy, aggressive race, perhaps because living was so precarious on those low, desolate coral rings where drinking water came only from coconuts and where fish and shellfish were the only protein and where none of the high-island vegetables would grow. The first Pomare gained a toehold in Tahiti by marrying the heiress of a small but independent district in the north of the island. Rhen, by persuading Cook and his successors (who had made Matavai Bay in the north their headquarters) that he was the king or at least the potential king, he waged war against the traditional chiefs. This was a long drawn-out process and one in which Tu himself did little fighting. The effectiveness of his power was owing almost entirely to the remnants of the Bounty, the nine mutineers and seven so-called innocents - sailors who had not joined the mutiny but whose skills were so valuable that Christian, leader of the rebels, had forced them to come with him.

The details of that phase of the famous mutiny (referred to above as little known but as of fateful consequence to the internal affairs of Tahiti) was virtually ignored until the publication of James Morrison's Journal in 1939. Morrison was Bligh's boatswain, a member of the "innocents" and an exceptionally articulate recorder of the events of approximately two years between the casting-off of Bligh and the imprisonment aboard H.M.S. Pandora of those left on Tahiti. The two bounty mutineers who acted virtually as mercenary officers in Tu's "army" were the notorious Churchill and Thompson, who had secured a good supply of muskets from the Bounty's store and whose professional training as royal Marines rendered the forces of the old chiefs of the Atehuru and the Teva almost helpless.

They were attacked separately and set against each other until by the end of a year or more of fighting, Tu was able to make a grand tour around the whole island with feasts and marae ceremonies featuring human sacrifices that terrified the populace and compelled obeisance from all the chiefs to his son. Everywhere the young Tu, later to become Pomare II, was invested with the maro ura or red girdle, this time fashioned out of the customary sacred red feathers but of the royal and ensign left behind by Wallis. Ironically it thus became a symbol of English support and of brutality.

By 1791 Tu's sway was virtually undisputed - in the strong arm or military sense, but never in the old hereditary social sense. Although he was merely an upstart to the legendary chiefs, Pomare was a tremendous man in physical stature, over six feet in height and weighing three hundred pounds, a powerful and terrifying figure in his heyday, but a dissolute, cruel, and self-serving ruler. Then one morning in the year 1803 he set out in his canoe in the harbor of Matavai to visit a British warship at anchor off shore. As he approached the ship he stood up to hail them, suddenly clutched his back, and fell precipitately into the canoe with his arms dangling lifeless over the sides. No one knew what caused this sudden death, but it was assumed that some internal convulsion, possibly kidney failure, had seized him.

He was succeeded by an even more power-hungry son, who named himself Pomare II in the European royal tradition at the age of about twenty-nine. Of course he the "kin g" was challenged and his fight for supremacy see-sawed over the next decade. He lost one critical battle and had to flee to Moorea for a year or more. But he shrewdly allowed himself to be converted to Christianity and thus won the support and (because of their fear of his opponents) sometimes the firearms of the missionaries. In a crucial battle with Tati, he defeated the great Teva clan in the south and then, instead of massacring them as was the old-time custom , he pardoned them and magnanimously clinched his supremacy. it was a calculated hypocrisy, and it worked.

Although he had professed conversion for at least two years, the missionaries had been distrustful of his ruthless character and were wary. They kept postponing action, but this unprecedented gesture of what they chose to see as Christian mercy won their consent. He was officially accepted into the church: all the sacred (and ethnologically priceless) idols were burned in great bonfires. The ancient religion was joyously obliterated or at least driven underground. At the height of his power in 1819 he promulgated the "Code of Pomare," transforming the sectarian life of the island to English law, as he had the spiritual; life to English religion. He then proceeded to drink himself to death in a gargantuan alcoholic binge that lasted for two years.

Tahiti Bounty

Beneath the island's volcanic pinnacles, the Bounty passed around the surf-pounded reef beyond Point Venus. Already she was hailed by throngs of canoes; and when Bligh called out that he had come from Britain,opr 'Pretanee', the delighted islanders swarmed onto the ship, 'and in ten Minutes,' wrote Bligh, 'I could scarce find my own people.'

The old-timers - Nelson, the gardener, William Peckover, the gunner, Armourer Joseph Coleman and Bligh himself - greeted and were greeted with warm recognition. The remainder of the crew now learned that the stories that had filled their ears throughout the long hard outward voyage - about the island's beauty, its sexually uninhibited women, its welcoming people - were not tall tales, or sailors' fantasy. Beyond the ship, its undulating slopes and valleys, gullies and dramatic peaks casting shifting green-blue shadows in the morning sun, rose the vision of Tahiti. Below, the blue sea round them was clogged with cheerful canoes that had come laden with gifts of plantains. coconuts and hogs.

And filling the deck, milling and laughing around them, wee the tall, clean-limbed, smooth-skinned Tahitians. The Bounty men - bowlegged, pockmarked, scarred and misshapen, toothless and, despite Bligh's best efforts, very dirty - regarded the improbably handsome, dark-haired islanders with both appetite and awe. Their brown skin gleaming with perfumed oil, garlanded with flowers, and flashing smiles with strong white teeth such as few Englishmen had ever seem, these superior men and women were also friendly and accessible. significantly, all cases of scurvy were quickly cured; even Morrison allowed 'that in a few days of arrival there was no appearance of sickness or disorder in the ship.'

The following day, 27 October, manoeuvring around canoes and people, Bligh successfully worked the Bounty into Matavai Bay, and dropped anchor. Under the escort of a chief named Poerno, Bligh was taken to Point Venus, the peninsula that formed the northeast point of Matavai Bay, from where in 1769 Cook had observed the transit of Venus. Standing under the graceful and now familiar coconut palms, the surf breaking against the lava-black beach, Bligh seems to have drawn a deep breath of happiness.

It had been Bligh's original plan to conceal Captain Cook's death from the Tahitians; Cook was held in such high esteem that a portrait of him, left as a gift eleven years earlier, was still in good repair. but some three months before the Bounty's arrival, another foreign ship - apparently the first since Cook's departure - had brought news of his terrible death at the hands of the Sandwich Islanders. nonetheless, David Nelson - with or without Bligh's prompting is unclear - introduced Bligh as 'Cook's son' to the local dignitaries; they are reported to have received this news with much satisfaction, although subsequent interactions suggest this was not perhaps taken b them as a literal truth

On 1 November, Bligh set out on a scouting trip to Oparre, a district to the west of Matavai. In order to uproot and carry off the large number of breadfruit he sought, he needed the permission of all the various chiefs with jurisdiction over the areas in which he would be working. A visit to pay his respects to the Ari'i Rahi, the six-year-old king of Oparre, took him inland towards the hills, through the delightful breadfruit flats of Oparre,' which wee cut by a serpentine river. In the course of the day the two parties entertained each other, The Tahitians offering an impromptu heiva, or dancing festival.

Bligh a demonstration of his pocket pistol. Before returning to his ship, Bligh contemplated the scenes of the day - the sparkling streams and green glades of the interior, and the dramatic sweep of the palm-rimmed lava beach of Matavai Bay. 'These two places,' he reflected, 'are certainly the Paradise of the World, and if happiness could result from situation and convenience, here it is to be found in the highest perfection. I have seen many parts of the World,' he continued in this remarkably personal entry, 'but Otaheite is capable of being preferable to them all.'

Tynah, the paramount chief of Matavai and the adjoining region, soon became the local dignitary with whom Bligh and his men had the most communion. He and his outgoing wife, Iddeeah, were both large, impressive persons, Tynah standing over six foot three and weighing some twenty-one stones. Now around thirty-seven years old, Tynah had been known to Cook and Bligh previously as 'Otoo'. Adroitly, Bligh conveyed to Tynah and the other lesser chiefs that the gift his sovereign, King George of Pretanee, would mot welcome in exchange for the gifts his ship carried was the breadfruit tree. Delighted that King George could be so easily satisfied, the chiefs readily gave their assent, and Bligh, much relieved, began to organize his land base.

The Admiralty's delay in getting Bligh his orders had ensured that the Bounty arrived in Tahiti near the outset of the western monsoon season, which ran from November to April, a period of rain and gales avoided by sailors. Additionally, as he had been directed to return by the Endeavour Straits, Bligh knew he had to await the eastern monsoon, which would begin at the end of April or early May; in short, the bounty would not e departing Tahiti until April, five months away, and several months longer than had originally been planned. On 2 November, Bligh sent a party to Point Venus that included William Peckover, Peter Haywood, four of the able seamen, as well as nelson the gardener and his assistant William Brown, all under the command of Fletcher Christian.

It was their job to establish and maintain the camp for the gardeners' word. Eventually two tents and a shed, built of bamboo poles and thatched with palm branches, were erected on Cook's old site and a boundary line drawn, 'within which none of the Natives were to enter without permission and all were cautioned against it.' The compound was to serve as a nursery where the transplanted breadfruit could be closely supervised befoe being transported to the Bounty. here, in the shade of the coconuts and breadfruit that rolled down to the dark shore, as palm fronds clattered and rustled in the sea breezes far above their heads, Christian and the rest of his small land party were to live and work for the next few months. Their less fortunate companions were expected to spend the night on board their ship.

Bligh himself divided his time between an anxious monitoring of his plants, and careful, if enjoyable, diplomacy. the success of his breadfruit operation depended upon the continued goodwill of such powerful friends as Poeno and Tynah (the father of the boy king), both of whom he knew from his former visit. Based upon his earlier experience, there was little reason to imagine this goodwill would in fact waver, but there was reason to fear the curiosity and acquisitiveness of the common man. So far, as Bligh had noted, the thefts of the Bounty had suffered had been insignificant, but he was keenly aware that this situation could quickly change. He had already had to administer the third flogging of the voyage, in this case twelve lashes to Alexander Smith, able seaman, 'for suffering the Gudgeon of the large Cutter to be drawn out without knowing it.' The flogging had horrified the watching Tahitians - especially the women, who, according to Bligh, 'showed every degree of Sympathy which marked them to be the most humane and affectionate creatures in the World.'

The temptation for Bligh to take personal advantage of his circumstances, to strike out on short expeditions, making discoveries and taking the surveys in which he was to expert, all to his own greater glory, must have been very great. But Bligh had virtually promised Banks a successful outcome to the voyage, and Banks had made it patently clear that he cared about nothing but breadfruit. The nursery, therefore, and everything that concerned the nursery, were to be the sole objects of his attention.

Bligh could not risk some fatal lapse of discipline, not, as it appears, could he trust his officers or men. this was most apparent in Bligh's attempt to regulate the ongoing torrent of trade between his ship and his island hosts. The establishment of a fixed market, as opposed to a free-for-all run by the sailors' whim, was of immediate advantage to his own ship, as well as to future British vessels. As Cook had done - and based closely on cook's own rules - Bligh drafted a set of injunctions intended to govern his men's conduct among the Tahitians:

1st. At the Society or Friendly Islands, no person whatever is to intimate that Captain Cook was killed by Indians or that he is dead.

2nd. No person is ever to speak, or give the least hint, that we have come on purpose to get the breadfruit plant, until I have made my plan known to the chiefs.

3rd. Every person is to study to gain the good will and esteem of the natives; to treat them with all kindness; and not to take from them, by violent means, any thing that they may have stolen; and no one is ever to fire, but in defence of his life.

4th. Every person employed on service, is to take care that no arms or implements of any kind under their charge, are stolen; the value of such thing, being lost, shall be charged against their wages.

5th. No man is to embezzle, or offer to sale, directly, or indirectly, any part of the King's stores, of what nature soever.

6th. A proper person or persons will be appointed to regulate trade, and barter with the natives; and no officer or seaman, or other person belonging to the ship, is to trade for any kind of provisions, or curiosities; but if such officer or seaman wishes to purchase any particular thing, he is to apply to the provider to do it for him. by this means a regular market will be carried on, and all disputes, which otherwise may happen with the natives will be avoided. All boats are to have everything handed out of them as sun-set.

These orders were nailed to the mizzenmast immediately upon anchoring - so Morrison reports, citing a garbled version of only item number six on Bligh's list. Bligh's orders, Morrison recalled, prohibited 'the Purchase of Curiosities or anything except Provisions,' adding that 'there were few or no instances of the order being disobeyed, as no curiosity struck the seamen so forcibly as a roasted pig....' Nevertheless, it was this last order that appears to have been responsible for the only complaints worth recording during the twenty-three weeks spent on Tahiti. Bligh's directive aimed to avoid the disputes that would inevitably arise if trade were conducted by forty-five individuals following no particular rules, and to ensure that, as commanding officer and purser, the could reliably provision his ship.

Captain Cook himself, who in the course of his ling career had been many a promising market ruined, had been very clear on this point: 'Thus, was the fine prospect we had of getting a plentifull supply of refreshments of these people frustrated,' Cook had lamented, after one of his men had volunteered a quantity of rare red feathers for a pig, inadvertently establishing red feathers as the currency for all future pigs. 'And which will ever be the case so long as every one is allowed to make exchanges for what he pleaseth and in what manner he please's.' Morrison undoubtedly understood Bligh's motivation for the directive, and John Fryer, as master, most certainly did. Yet Morrison complain ed that when the trade in hogs began to slacken, 'Mr. Bligh seized on all that came to the ship big & small.

Deal or alive, taking them as his property, and serving them as the ship's allowance at one pound per Man per Day.' According to Morrison, Fryer also complained to Bligh, apparently publicly, that his property was being taken. The site designated for trade was one of the tents at the nursery compound, where the boundary market kept crowds at bay. William Peckover had been placed in charge, a sensible choice given his knowledge of Tahitian language and customs picked up in the course of several visits he had made to the island with Cook. Nonetheless, the sailors continued to encourage their Tahitian friends to come to the ship surreptitiously.

'The Natives observing that the Hog were seized as soon as they Came on board ... became very shy of bringing a hog in sight of Lieut. Bligh,' Morrison reports and islanders conspired to trick their commanding officer. the Tahitian 'watched all opportunity when he was on shore to bring provisions to their friends.' Not for the first time - and certainly for the last - Bligh must have wished for the support of even a small party of marines, armed sentinels who would have stood apart from the fraternity of seamen, and whose loyalty to his commands he could have counted on when his back was turned.

Despite Morrison's lengthy complaint, time passed pleasantly enough for the seamen who were entrusted with minimal duties and allowed on-shore regularly [for refreshment'. Joseph Coleman set up a forge to make and repair goods for the ship and islanders alike. The usual wooding parties were sent off to cut timber, while others prepared puncheons of salted pork for the return journey. the great cabin was refitted for the pots waiting in the land nursery, only, as Bligh logged, 'the Carpenter running a Nail through his Knee very little was done.' Charles Norman, a carpenter's mate, had been ill for several days with a complaint diagnosed by Huggan variously as rheumatism and 'Peripneumonianotha', and the quatermaster's mate, George Simpson, also according to Huggan, had 'Cholera Morbus', Bligh bought a mulch goat for

Norman, believing its milk would help the patient's chronic diarrhoea. the men recovered and Bligh was able to report a clean sick list, save that the 'Venereal list is increased to four'; sadly, the European disease was now endemic.

Bligh met almost every day with Tynah and his family and retinue, and each day he logged some new discovery abut his hosts' culture. along with the ship's officers, he was entertained by lascivious heivas, in which the women, 'according to the horrid custom,' distorted their faces into obscene expressions. He discussed the tradition of infanticide among the flamboyant arioi, and he recorded the recipe for delicious pudding made from a turnip-like root. One day. Bligh engaged in long theological enquiry, in which he was questioned closely about his own beliefs: who was the son and who was the wife of his God? Who ws his father and mother? Who was before your God and where is he? Is he in the winds or in the sun? When asked about childbirth in his country, Bligh answered as well as he was able, and enquired in turn how this was done in Tahiti. Queen Iddeeah replied by mimicking a woman in labour, squatting comfortably to her heels between the protective arms of a male attendant who stroked her belly. Iddeeah was vastly amused on learning of the difficulties of Pretanee's women.

'Let them to this & not fear,' she told Bligh, who appears to have been persuaded by this tender pantomime. In the evenings, Bligh entertained his hosts on board the Bounty, which none seemed to tire of visiting. As Tynah's royal status forbade him to put food or drink into his own mouth, Bligh himself sometimes served as cupbearer if attendants were unavailable; Iddeeah, according to custom, ate apart from the men. After the meals, the company lounged lazily around the small deck area, enjoying the offshore breezes, and the muffled pounding of the surf on shore and reef, and the lap of the waves below. Not infrequently, Bligh's guests stayed the night on board the Bounty, loth to depart.

How Bligh passed his time at Tahiti, can be followed, day by day, event by event, as recorded in his fulsome log. What is not known with any clarity is how time was passed onshore. All midshipmen were required to keep up their own logs, to be produced at such time as they applied to pass for lieutenant, and one would give much to have Fletcher Christian's. As it is, life at Point Venus can be sketched only in broad outline. Every evening, when the work of the shore party was winging down, the Tahitians gathered at 'the Post' before sunset. almost all of the Bounty men had found taios, or protective friends, who took them into their homes and families.

At least to of the men, George Stewart from the Orkneyhs and, perhaps less predictably, the critical

James Morrison, had women friends to whom they were particularly attached, while all the men seemed to have enjoyed regular sexual partners; whether or not Fletcher Christian had formed an attachment to any one woman was to become a hotly contested question - at the very least, he, like young Peter Heywood, had to be treated for 'venereals'. The women of Tahiti, as Bligh would later famously write, were 'handsome, mild and cheerful in their manners and conversation, possessed of great sensibility and have sufficient delicacy to make them admired and beloved.' They were also by European standards not only very beautiful, but sexually uninhibited and experienced in ways that amazed and delighted their English visitors.

'Even the mouths of Women are not exempt from the pollution, and many other as uncommon ways have they of gratifying their beastly inclinations,' as Bligh had observed, aghast. Famously, favours of the

Tahitian women could be purchased for mere nails. both on ship and at the camp, Bligh allowed female guests to stay the night, at the same time trying, through Ledward, his assistant surgeon, to keep track of the venereal diseases. When dusk came, the shore party were left more or less to their own devices. The sundown gatherings brought entertainments - wrestling matches, dances and games, feasts, martial competitions - but also a sexual privacy, even a domesticity, not allowed to the men still on board ship. From the curving arm of Point Venus, Christian and his companions could look back towards Matavai Bay, past the bounty riding gently at anchor, to the darkening abundance of trees that seemed to cascade from the grave, unassailable heights of the island.

As the weeks passed, the potted plants began to fill the nursery tent, and by the end of November, some six hundred wee 'in a very fine way'. meanwhile, other ship duties wee intermittently carried on. Bligh ordered the sails brought onshore, where they were aired and dried under Christian's supervision. the large cutter was found to have a wormy bottom and had to be cleaned and repainted, under the shade of a large awning that Bligh had made to protect the workmen from the sun. these duties were accompanied by the usual problems. Mathew Thompson was flogged with a dozen lashes 'for insolence and disobedience of Orders'. Also, Bligh logged, 'by the remissness of my Officers & People at the Tent,' a rudder was stolen, the only theft, as Bligh observed, so far, of any consequence; the officer in charge of the tent was of course Fletcher Christian. there is no record of punishment.

Most seriously, Purcell once again had begun to balk at his orders. When asked to make a whetstone for one of the Tahitian men, he refused point-blank, claiming that to do so would spoil his tools. On this occasion, at last, Bligh punished the carpenter with confinement to his cabin - although, as he recorded, he did not intend to lose the use of him, but to remit him to his duty to Morrow.' towards the end of November, strong winds began to accompany what had become daily showers of rain, and by early December the dark weather brought an unfamiliar, heavy well.

The Bounty rolled uncomfortably at her anchorage, while the surf breaking on Dolphin Bank, the outlying reef, had become violent. On 6 December, Bligh described a scene 'of Wind and Weather which I never supposed could have been met with in this place.' From midnight until well into the morning, amid torrents of rain, a foaming was agitated the ship 'in a most tremendous manner'. Onshore, Christian's party was cut off by the swelling of the nearby river and an alarming influx of the sea. In the morning. Tynah and Iddeeah fought their way to the Bounty in canoes through a sea so high that, as Bligh wrote, 'I could not have supposed any Boat could have existed a moment.'

On board, the couple offered their tearful greetings, saying they had believed the ship lost in the night. The rainy season, which Europeans had never experienced before, had commenced, and it was at once clear that Matavai Bay was no longer a feasible anchorage. The plants had been threatened by salt spray as the winds and high sea raged, and Bligh was determined to move them to safer ground as soon as he was able. On Nelson's advice, he delayed an immediate departure until plants in an apparently dormant state showed signs of being alive and healthy.

some days after the storm, Huggan, the quondam surgeon, at last succumbed to his 'drunkenness and indolence'. 'Exercise was a thing he could not bear an Idea of,' Bligh wrote by way of an epitaph. since his death had been projected even before the Bounty departed Depford Dockyard, Huggan had a good run for his money. He was buried the following day to the east of Point Venus, across the river that cut the point and not far from the sea. 'There the Sun rises,' Tynah said as the grave was being dug, 'and there it sets, and here you may bury Terronnoo, for so he was called.' Joining Huggan's shipmates for the funeral were all the chiefs of the region and a great many other people, respectful and solemn for the surgeon and a great many other people, respectful and solemn for the surgeon's perhaps undeservedly dignified rites. Huggan was only the second European to be buried on the island.

It was Christmas by the time the dormant plants had put forth the desired shoots, and the men began the cumbersome task of moving camp. A reef harbour at Oparre, to the west of Matavai, had been chosen as the Bounty's new anchorage. With a watchful eye on the weather which had continued to be troubled, Bligh ordered the bounty readied for her short journey, and had his 774 potted breadfruit plants carefully carried on board. At half past ten in the morning, the ship weighted anchor and cautiously set out to follow the launch, which was carrying the tents and which Bligh had sent ahead as a pilot. The second camp, according to Bligh was 'a delightful situation in every respect.' The ship lay in sheltered, smooth water, where the tide lapped at the beach and no surf broke. Dense stands of trees, shaded the new nursery, which was established along he same lines as the Matavai camp with the addition of a hut supplied by Tynah. Tynah, who had lobbied hard not to lose the Bounty and all the amusements and lucrative trade she brought, was delighted with the relocation, as he also had jurisdiction of Oparre. Taios left behind were still close enough to visit, and the easy social routine that had been enjoyed at Matavai was soon resumed, with people promenading along the beach opposite the ship 'every fair Evening'. Bligh diretg4d the ship 'to be laid up and everything put below' in part so as to avoid more thefts, but this was also a sign that the men on board could look forward to only perfunctory duties.

Nonetheless, the very day the plants and ship were safely re-established, Bligh had William Muspratt, the cook's assistant, flogged with a dozen lashes for 'neglect of duty'. Two days later Robert Lamb, the butcher, was also flogged with a dozen 'for suffering his Cleaver to be Stolen'. This now brought the total number of men punished up to six. Although the temperature remained warm, this new season brought torrential rain and squalls, and skies so dense with sodden clouds that for an entire moth Bligh was unable to take a single celestial observation. it was on one of these dark, impenetrable nights that three of the Bounty's men deserted. When the watch was relieved at four in the morning of 5 January 1789. Charles Churchill, the master-at-arms, John Millward, able seaman, and William Muspratt, who had only recently been flogged, were found missing. gone with them were the small cutter along with eight stands of arms and cartouches of ammunition.

Bligh responded to the news with an icy resolve that he had hitherto not displayed. to his Tahitian friends, he stated in very clear, straightforward and polite language that he expected the men returned. Laughing nervously, they asked Bligh if he would hold them hostage on board his ship, as cook had done. this was an unexpected and revealing question. In 1769, during his first to Tahiti, Cook had lost two marines to desertion and had retaliated by holding the chiefs hostage, his rationale being that his men could not survive on the island without the complicity of the islanders. that Bligh's friends raised this concern twenty years after the vent suggests that Cook's action had left a deep impression. Bligh reassured his friends that he would not resort to such a stratagem, adding, in his log, that he had 'never shown any violence or Anger' at any of the petty thefts that had occurred and had enjoyed such mutual goodwill that he knew his friends had confidence in him, and that he had 'therefore no doubt but they will bring the Deserters back' - but, if they should not, eh would 'make the whole Country Suffer for it.' Having issued his warnings, there was little Bligh could do but wait, relying on local intelligence to flush out the fugitives.

That some of his men would try to desert probably did not take Bligh completely by surprise; again, he had his experience with cook to draw upon. Cook had suffered desertions on Tahiti during all three of his expeditions. Recognizing that the inducements to leave ship were many, Cook had summoned his crew and lectured them at length on the 'spirit of Desertion', informing them that 'they Might run off if they pleased,' as one of the company later recorded, 'but they might Depend upon it he would Recover them again.' Stern as it was, the speech did not deter other, also futile attempts. Some years later, on learning of the Bounty's fate,

James Matra, a midshipman on cook's first journey, would report to Banks the astonishing news that a mass desertion had been planned by 'most of the People' and some of the gentlemen of the Endeavour Mr. Midshipman Matra had been instrumental in dissuading them, so he would claim, his principal line of argument being that the men could be certain of 'dying rotten' of the pox if they were to live out their lives on the island.

Within his own company, Bligh must have seen evidence that his officers and people were settling down into Tahitian life and adopting local customs, most visibly in their passion for being tattooed. the first tattoos had arrived in England with sailors returning from the American or the Pacific, and especially from the Endeavour (with Joseph Banks) at the end of cook's first voyage, when they had become tokens of great prestige. The Bounty's company tastes were varied, some sticking conservatively to English iconography. James Morrison, of all people, for reasons only to be guessed at, had had himself tattooed with the order of the Garter around his leg and the Knights of the Garter's motto: 'Honi soit qui mal y pense' - 'Shame on him who evil thinks.' Thomas Ellison wore simply his name and 'October 25th 1788' on his right arm - the date he had first sighted Otaheite.

But several of the men had undergone traditional Tahitian tattooing over large parts of their body, particularly on their buttocks. In Tahiitan tradition, a man was not eligible to marry unless ha had undergone the lengthy and painful operation of having his entire backside b lacked over. Bligh left descriptions only of the mutineers, and with one exception (John mills, the Scottish gunner's mate) every one of them was tattooed, and usually 'very much tatowed' or 'tatowed in several places . Peter Heywood was in this company, being 'very much tattowed', among other things with the three-legged emblem of the Isle of Man. those who had received the elaborate tattoos of Tahitian manhood included George Steward, Matthew Quintal and Fletcher Christian.

Still Bligh himself had encouraged friendly relations with the Tahitians, and his men's enthusiasm for the more eye-catching aspects of their culture was not something to be readily, or fruitfully, legislated. but now, as he conducted his own grim investigation of the events, he made other discoveries. On examination of the men's personal effects for clues, a piece of paper was found inside Charles Churchill's chest on which he had written his own name and the names of three of the shore party. the deserters would later say darkly that 'many others intended to remain among the islands,' and making a list of men committed to an illegal act such as desertion or mutiny - was an old trick.

When Captain Edward Edwards, back in his happier days before he captained the Pandora, had thwarted the mutinous plot on board his ship Narcissus, a list of names of the men involved in the plot had been discovered on one of the would-be mutineers; perhaps the rash act of committing a name to paper was perceived as a kind of security that bound the man in question t tone's cause.

Some years later, in personal correspondence, Bligh reported that 'this List had Christian, Heywood and several other Names in it,' and that he had approached his protege 'not conceiving Christian could be guilty of such a thing, and who, when I showed it to him, laughed as well as myself.' To a man, the shore party professed their innocence to Bligh, and 'denyd it so firmly, that He was inclined from Circumstances to believe them and said no more to them about it,' according to Morrison.

In the official log no mention is made of this mysterious list; Bligh's personal log, in which he would have been most expected to have made some remarks about the event, ends on 23 October, and does not resume until 5 April 1789; a comprehensive index, in Bligh's own handwriting, is all that can be found of the missing potion. the official log, submitted to the Admiralty, makes no mention of his suspicious whatsoever and shows Bligh's professionalism at its best. If the men had convinced him of their innocence, then he was bound to 'say no more about it.' Or was the incident omitted for more self-serving reasons - because later evens proved he had been duped? At least 'three of the Party on shore' would remain among the mutineers: Peter Heywood, William Brown and Fletcher Christian.

One curious and generally unremarked incident occurred four days after Churchill and his companions deserted. As Bligh reported, 'one of the officers on shore' cut a branch of an oil-nut tree growing at a marae, or sacred site, and, 'accidently bringing it into the dwelling where my people are at, all the Natives both Men and Women suddenly left.' The branch had tabooed the shore hut, no Tahitian would set foot here until the appropriate ceremony lifted the taboo. Curiously, however, as Bligh noted, 'when I came on shore I found a branch of this Tree tyed to one the Posts, altho they saw the effect it had of keeping the Natives from the House.' Is it significant that in the immediate aftermath of the desertion one of the officers - Christian or Heywood - tabooed the house in which three men implicated on Churchill's list happened to live? Was this a sign to Tahitian taios and allies to stay away, perhaps in the wake of an aborted plot? A whimsical amulet to ward off further trouble? Or, as Bligh clearly believed, more happenstance?

Ade Pearson

The Tahitian Royal Family

The year 1791 saw the kingdom of greater Tahiti came into being, It was in that year, a junior chief, Out Vairatoa, succeeded in uniting the disparate chiefdoms of Tahiti, Moorea, Meetia and the Tetiaroa group into a single entity. He assumed the title of King of Tahiti, and was known by various names, history finally settling on Pomare (little cough). Pomare I's descendants eventually succeeded to the other High Chiefdoms through successful political marriages and inheritance. Pomare IV inherited the Ra'iatea chiefdom in 1857. She had already married the hereditary Chief of Bora Bora, and united his domains with her own, on his death in 1860.

Prior to that, the ancient Kingdom of Tahiti originally comprised four separate principalities. Tahiti proper, consisting of Tahiti, Moorea, Meetia and the Tetiaroa group. Huahine, comprising Huahine proper and Tupemanu. Ra'iatea, comprising the islands of Ra'iatea and Tahaa. Bora Bora, comprising the islands of Bora Bora proper, Motuiti, Maupiti and Mapateia. The High Chiefs of all these islands descend from the High Chief Hiro. He had two sons, Hoatatama of Ra'iatea and Haneti of Bora Bora, founders of the dynasties of Maro'ura (the Red Centre) and Marotea (the White Centre). The island of Tahiti was divided into three great chiefdoms, Papara, Pare and Attahuru, the most powerful ruler of which was also king of the entire island. As soon as a male heir was born to one of these rulers, he became Chief, and his father became regent on his behalf.

The attempt at colonization by the Spaniards in 1774 was followed by the settlement of thirty persons brought in 1797 by the missionary ships "Duff." Though befriended by Pomare I. (who lived till 1805), they had many difficulties, especially from the constant wars, and at length they fled with Pomare II. to Eimeo and ultimately to New South Wales, returning in 1812, when

In 1815 Pomare II regained his power in Tahiti, for a time the missionaries made good progress and a printing press was established (1817), and coffee, cotton and sugar were planted (1819); but soon there came a serious relapse into heathen practices and immorality.

Pomare II. died of drink in 1824. His successor, Pomare III., died in 1827, and was succeeded by his half-sister Aimata, the unfortunate "Queen Pomare (IV.)." In 1828 a new fanatical sect, the "Mamaia," arose, which gave much trouble to the missions. The leader proclaimed that he was Jesus Christ, and promised to his followers a sensual paradise. In 1836 the French Catholic missionaries in Mangareva attempted to open a mission in Tahiti.

Queen Pomare, advised by the English missionary and consul, Pritchard, refused her consent, and removed by force two priests who had landed surreptitiously and to whom many of the opposition party in the state had rallied. In 1838 a French frigate appeared, under the command of Abel Dupetit-Thouars, and extorted from Pomare the right of settlement for Frenchmen of every profession. Pritchard opposed this, and caused Pomare to apply for British protection; but this was a failure, and the native chiefs compelled the queen, against her will, to turn to France.

A convention was signed in 1843, placing the islands under French protection, the authority of the queen and chiefs being expressly reserved. Dupetit-Thouars now reappeared, and, alleging that the treaty had not been duly carried out, deposed the queen and took possession of the islands. His high-handed action was not countenanced by the French government; but while, on formal protest from England, it professed not to sanction the annexation, it did not retrace the steps taken. Two years spent in reducing the party in the islands opposed to French rule; an attempt to conquer the westerns islands failed; and at length, by agreement with England, France promised to return to the plan of a protectorate and leave the western islands to their rightful owners.

Pomare IV died in 1877, and her son Ariane (Pomare V.) abdicated in 1880, handing over the administration to France, and in the same year Tahiti, was proclaimed a French colony. In 1903 the whole of the French establishment in the Eastern Pacific were declared on colony, and the then existing elective general council was superseded by the present administration.

www.ingramcontent.com/pod-product-compliance
Lightning Source LLC
Chambersburg PA
CBHW021102080526
44587CB00010B/346